NORN LUP?

A Journey of Railways, Roads and Wats

Christmas 2013

Rachel Beswetherick

Definition: *Norn Lup* (นอนหลับ) – **sleep**

(The Rough Guide Phrasebook Thai)

For Stan ...
we walked in memory of you

and dedicated to Rohan ...
because family matters more than anything else

Cover Design by Jonathon Maxwell

ISBN 978-1-291-32425-9

CONTENTS

ROUTE FROM BAN PONG TO SANGKHLA BURI

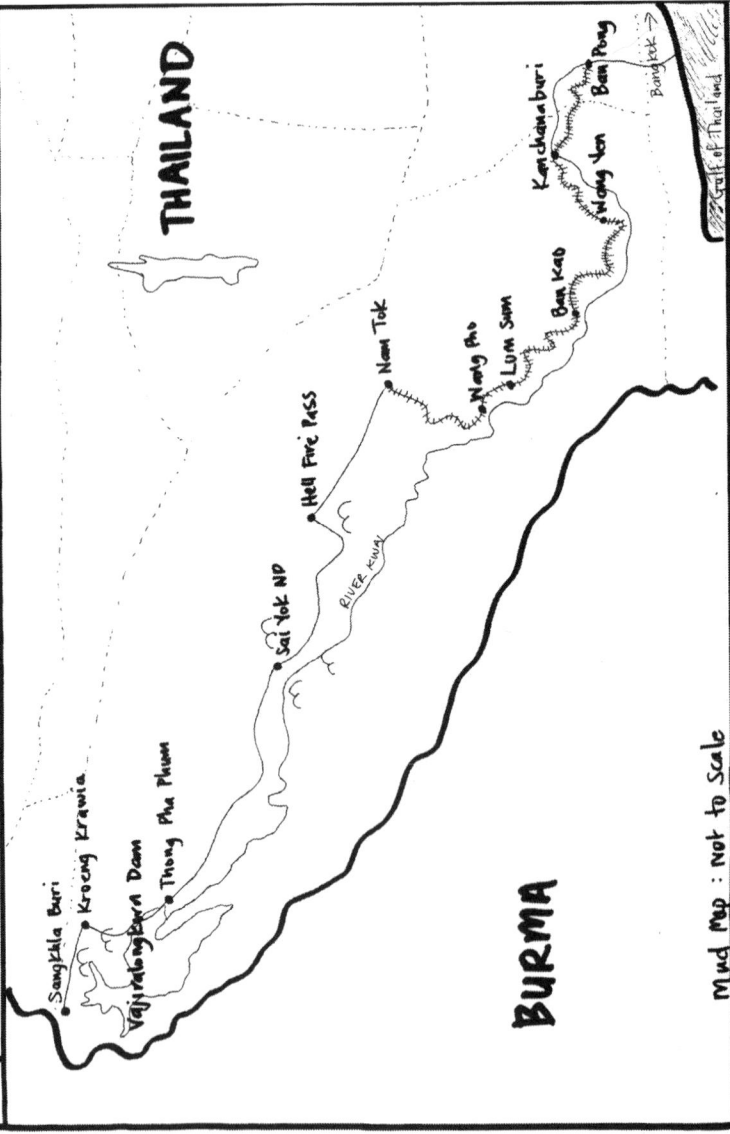

THAILAND

BURMA

Sangkhla Buri
Kroeng Krawia
Vajiralongkorn Dam
Thong Pha Phum

Sai Yok NP

Hell Fire Pass

RIVER KWAI

Nam Tok

Wang Pho
Lum Sum
Ban Kao

Kanchanaburi
Wang Yen
Ban Pong

Bangkok →

Gulf of Thailand

Mud Map : not to Scale

Prologue

"I'm looking for the unexpected.
I'm looking for things I've never seen before."
Robert Mapplethorpe

I have just found a 'Kinder' egg on the back pew of a church. I am not surprised. My boyfriend, Tom, is always hiding these for me to find. The tiny Spanish style church is situated on the outskirts of Ross-on-Wye, the town where tourism began in Britain. It's a pleasant summer's day in the English countryside. The sun is shining. We both sit on a bench in the grounds of the church looking out on the green rolling hills that stretch all the way to the horizon. I crush the 'Kinder' egg, eager to eat the chocolate and see what the toy is inside. Tom is noticeably excited about the toy. I don't think anything of it. Inside the egg is the familiar yellow plastic egg-shaped box. I open it and inside is a ring. I'm confused. Then it hits me — it's not the toy that 'Kinder' originally put inside this egg. It has been tampered with. I look up and Tom is down on one knee — "Will you marry me Rachel?" I don't hesitate. I know exactly what I want.

Back in London we share our exciting news with Tom's

family and then set about making Skype calls to my family back in Australia. We manage to call everyone – except my brother Luke. Luke and I have been planning an expedition. Although I have just got engaged, I am keen to continue pursuing this dream of ours. Tom understands this. It's why I love him. He understands who I am and how I work.

I finally manage to reach Luke and tell him our news. He is excited for us. I promise him that even though Tom and I are planning to marry as soon as possible, this will not change our plans for the expedition. This eagerness to marry is an unexpected desire. I am used to traveling the world alone, taking care of myself. This is a new feeling, wanting to be in someone else's care.

I am independent. Always have been. I've travelled solo to every continent and done some crazy things along the way. Five weeks on expedition with my brother, without Tom? I'll be fine, I think.

1

An Idea is Born

"An idea that is developed and put into action
is more important than an idea that exists only as an idea."
Siddhartha Buddha

I had always been a risk taker. Even as kids my two brothers (Luke and Rohan) and I would always be scheming hair-raising pursuits. Luckily our mother didn't know what we were up to: screeching down 45° angle roads on our bikes, scaling trees that required oxygen tanks to reach the top and jumping so high on trampolines that one day Luke suffered from concussion and couldn't remember walking home. In fact, when I look back, a lot of our shenanigans were either encouraged or instigated by Luke. As a six year old, Luke was launching himself off ski jumps that only advanced skiers would dare attempt. Much to our mother's dismay, Luke has never exhibited fear of any kind. Luke's risk taking always resulted in testing his physical limits. It eventually resulted in his being told at the age of twenty that he had a stress fracture in his spine. It seemed Luke was *not* invincible after all.

As a child I craved acceptance. I knew I was different. My mum dolled me in frilly dresses but behind the frills a little girl desperately wanted to get her hands dirty. As an older sister with two younger brothers close in age to each other, I spent a lot of time on my own. I'd create my own worlds where I was an explorer. My adventures took me on journeys to wild lands far away searching for the person I knew was inside me. Then one day I found her. Dad was the one who introduced me to walking. Mum not so keen on the physical activity, would stay at home. My brothers and I, handkerchiefs twisted onto our heads to protect us from the rain, felt invincible as we explored the terrain of the Blue Mountains like the pioneering explorers before us. Walking allowed that little girl in frills to discover who she really was – a lady of the land.

Entering my twenties, my imagination was replaced with reality. I was known as a *risk taker* by my friends and family. The imaginary worlds I'd created as a child were long gone. Now I was going on real, wild adventures around the world. At the age of twenty three I quit my 9 to 5 job and moved to South Africa to live in a small rural village called Phuthaditjhaba, five hours from Johannesburg. This is when my life began. I was doing what I'd always wanted to do: travel, explore and experience new places. After six months in Phuthaditjhaba, I then travelled throughout Central and South America where I saved turtles in Costa Rica and escaped from erupting volcanoes in Ecuador.

I also have an abundance of stories from my days living and working as a tour leader in South East Asia, such as losing a Slovenian woman in the chaos of Kuala Lumpur; leaving my twelve passengers stranded in Kota Bharu because I bought the wrong bus tickets; climbing Mount Kinabalu, at 4095m above sea level, with severe diarrhoea. So I guess you could say, when we announced to our friends and family that Luke and I were embarking on an expedition to do something that hadn't been done before, no one was surprised. Luke and I are anything but *normal*. My idea of a good time is activities that will make my heart race; adrenaline is my friend. I'm most comfortable hanging off a cliff or jumping out of a plane. I crave opportunities to take me beyond my limits. Luke is strongly influenced by the things he sees and hears. Inspired by Jim Carrey, Fawlty Towers' Basil Fawlty and Seinfeld's Kramer, his impersonations of them are spot on. To complement his wit, is a deep and thoughtful side. Underneath our exteriors we could both be described as deep, deep thinkers.

The older I got the more I wanted to do something ... crazy. I'd spent my younger years being inspired by explorers of the new world such as Christopher Columbus and present day adventurers such as Bear Grylls. As a young adult, still their escapades make my heart beat rapidly; my eyes open wide and my mind start to dream. So, early in 2010 when Luke and I decided we would do an expedition together, it stirred a side of me that had lain dormant for years. Our childhood escapades were continuing on into our adulthood. I could release my imagination out of the box I had stuffed it into years ago. I was finally going to realize my dream of doing something *crazy*, and we had the whole world to choose from! I was living in London and I'd spent the past two years enduring the UK's bitterly cold winters and borderline summers. The lack of sun had taken its toll on me and I'd suffered a mild bout of depression. I knew that a new challenge and some exposure to sun was just what I needed.

Conversations about the expedition were by Skype to bridge the 16,997km separating London and Sydney. Discovering quickly that coming up with an 'idea' was much harder than expected, hours of Skype calls were focused on the question – What should we do?

"What I really want to do is inspire others, through whatever we do," Luke said.

"I totally agree. What we do should be different and unique. I've found myself saying a number of times this year 'I need to do something crazy'," I replied.

"We could cycle across Australia?" Luke suggested.

"I'd be up for that! Actually I've been thinking of walking or cycling the length of the UK," I said, knowing I was pretty much up for anything.

"We could even do something like start an NGO or make a documentary," Luke said.

"It would be cool to do something in another country, like say Africa!" I said excited at the possibility of returning to the continent I love so much.

Conversation went back and forth like this for months. Lake Victoria in Africa was mentioned. Maybe we could do something there? Cycle around it? We weren't sure. We started to explore this idea. But then one day I received an email from Luke and everything changed.

14 August 2010

Rachel!

Hold your horses!!! (ie. Hold what you're currently looking into) I think I may have a good idea! Scroll down below ... and see what your initial thought is ...

>
>
>
>
>
>
>
>
>
>
>
>
>

The Burma-Thailand Railway! Also known as the Death Railway.

The reason that it's good is: I made a documentary about this when I did Stan's story! You made the music for it! We can (kind of) redo/retrace what Stan did.

It would make good sense to do it because we have an emotional and practical connection to it 'cause of Stan. This was something that was actually a part of our lives ... we have a connection to this. Even so, it doesn't have to be all about Stan and the war, but endurance etc ... whatever.

It's about 450km. Might be a few issues with the track being grown over and partly cut off but we can go around, and not even necessarily follow the whole track.

What do you think?

Luke

What did I think? I love Thailand! As a kid I'd frolicked on the beaches; been fascinated by the rats scurrying through the markets; arrived home with hair in braids, brightly coloured beads clinking at the end of each one. As a tour leader I'd cherished my days where I called work a day lazing by the beach, a sweaty hike in the jungle, or a contemplative stroll through a temple. Thailand fascinated me. Travelling in Thailand had, as yet, only allowed me to see what the typical tourist sees – smoggy cities, over populated towns and tropical islands. I'd ridden elephants, tubed down rivers, snorkelled over coral killed by heedless travellers but I'd never ventured into the *real* Thailand.

Over the past ten years Thailand had become one of the hottest holiday destinations in the world. Party goers and holiday seekers from all over the globe travelled to Thailand daily to enter a Utopia. For many tourists the Thailand they see is from the constraints of a fancy resort with cocktails in the pool, massages by the beach and *spaghetti bolognese* at the restaurant. Unfortunately for others, Utopia turns into a nightmare: injury or death by riding a motorbike whilst intoxicated; experiencing first hand Thailand's zero tolerance for drugs; or being robbed at an infamous *full moon party*. Every year more than one hundred Australian tourists die in Thailand and a similar number are arrested and detained in a Thai gaol for drug trafficking. Thailand can be very unforgiving. The opportunity to see the Thai people living in their own culture was too good to pass up.

It was obvious that Luke had stumbled across a winner of an idea. It made so much sense. This wasn't just an idea, it was a vision, a story, and we were already a part of it. We'd journeyed part of the way during Luke's making of a documentary called 'Still Standing'. Stan was a friend of ours who, as a Prisoner of War during WWII, had worked on the construction of the Thai-Burma Railway. The documentary had been born out of Luke's passion to tell Stan's story. I had composed the music. The journey we had taken with Stan had been eye-opening. This would be the next part of that journey. This idea had potential.

We began researching the Death Railway route. During my research I came across Rod Beattie, the curator and Managing Director of the Thai Burma Railway Centre in Kanchanaburi. Rod had spent over ten years researching the Thai-Burma Railway. In fact he had researched the fate of every single allied prisoner of war who had died as a result of working on the Death Railway. Families could now, on request, find out what had happened to a loved one all those years ago. He seemed like the perfect person to contact so I emailed him and got an interesting response.

31 August 2010

Dear Rachel,

You are not the first one to think of such an expedition. The only group to succeed was the London Police Expeditions Club about ten years ago. Their trek took three weeks but this expedition did not trek much of the railway.

There is no such thing as a 'continuous' route of the original railway except for the section from Nong Pladuk to Nam Tok (about 70km up country from Kanchanaburi) where the railway still runs.

Thereafter, the jungle has re-claimed much of it. The original route frequently disappears under private agricultural land, current roads and even under water for about 40km where a large dam was built in the 1980s.

About a quarter of the railway was in Burma and virtually all of the applicable area is out of bounds and inaccessible to foreign visitors. Also, as you may know, the railway did not follow a road but largely followed the Kwai Noi River, so there is no parallel land route to act as a guide for current day trekking and the current highway that travels in the general direction in Thailand is well away from the original railway for much of its length but sometimes close to it (or on top of it) although you have no way of knowing when and where without an extensive study.

Without detailed research and extensive

exploration most of its actual location is not easily found and/or the route not known.

The other thing to consider is that there were 688 bridges built along the 415 km of railway between the two countries and, except for those on the still working section of railway in Thailand, they are all gone. This means that ravines, watercourses, swamps etc have reverted to their original state and any of the route able to be located and not covered by impenetrable jungle is in relatively short sections anyway.

Many of the working groups at the time did not follow long distances of railway but worked on small sections (up to 8km) before being transported (although some walking if necessary) by river, road or rail.

To visit the actual campsites and/or find the route of the railway (to the extent possible) you will need knowledgeable guidance and to be taken to the locations separately. Within certain sections it is possible to do some trekking over a few km at a time, but to know where these areas are requires a detailed and informed understanding of the railway route as it stands now.

You mention journeying with Stan during the filming of the documentary. I assume that Stan was with F Force. If this is correct then it may be worth considering retracing the F Force march (as much as possible) and telling this story.

My initial exploration of the railway took about

four and a half years and there were areas that I could not penetrate. I have slowly explored these 'missed' areas during the succeeding twelve years and continue doing so today.

I hope this initial reply gives you a little more of an idea of what is here.

Yours sincerely,

Rod Beattie

At first reading, the email seemed disheartening. We were not going to be able to follow the 415km railway route. But pondering Rod's words "... it may be worth considering retracing the F Force march (as much as possible) and telling this story ..." took us beyond our initial thinking. Further research told us that the infamous F Force march had been a 300km, seventeen day forced trek from Ban Pong in Thailand to the Burma border. Our string of ideas had finally been strung into one great idea. The Death Railway Expedition was born: following a 300km route through Thailand in memory of the F Force and Stan who were forced to march. It fitted all the criteria – it was personal, it was unique, it was in honour of others, and it was definitely ... a little crazy!

The craziness of it didn't deter me. It only egged me on. I wanted to see what I was capable of. Part of the reason for pursuing an expedition of extreme measures was because I wanted to be put to the test. I knew that this would be the ultimate challenge. Walking 300km through Thailand, I would be at the mercy of things beyond my control. I would be forced to have confidence in myself. I would have to trust in my capabilities. I would have to have faith in my brother. At this stage I could only hope that I would have the strength physically, mentally and emotionally to walk day after day.

2

Departures and Arrivals

"We rarely know what it is we are seeking when we set out,
and even if we do, it is not often what
we end up finding."
Ingrid Emerick

Nine months later and it is now time to leave London and fly to Thailand – The Land of Smiles. A lot has happened during these months. As well as preparing for the expedition I got married! Strangely enough, my new husband and I actually met in South East Asia back in 2008. I'd been working as a tour leader for an Australian tour company leading trips through Thailand, Malaysia and Singapore. Tom was one of my passengers. We spent two weeks getting to know each other on the tour and becoming wildly smitten. What followed was seven months of separation where we built our relationship over Skype. I soon decided to quit my job and move to the UK so that we could give our relationship the dedication it deserved. Two years in the UK and then we were married at the end of my working holiday visa. The story of our meeting, dating and getting married is enough for another book. So, three years later here I am, married to Tom, and about to head back to Thailand, the place where our story began, without him.

It is departure day. We have been married a mere two months and one week. Married life has been a joy so far. We honeymooned in Morocco and are now living with a quirky Chinese couple in south east London. As I pack and prepare to leave I am surprised at our composure. There are no tears, yet. Tom has organised a *guy night* with his mates and is practically pushing me out the door so he can immerse himself in an evening of testosterone – which means – 'Call of Duty', beer and meat. We spend our final half hour together watching YouTube videos. Neither of us vocalise it but I know that we are both finding these final moments before the impending farewell awkward and uncomfortable. If there are things that are meant to be said at a time like this, we aren't saying them. YouTube allows us to ignore the inevitable words that need to be spoken – *'See you later.'*

I'm reminded of something Gilda Radner once said, 'I wanted a perfect ending. Now I've learned, the hard way, that some poems don't rhyme, and some stories don't have a clear beginning, middle, and end. Life is about not knowing, having to change, taking the moment and making the best of it, without knowing what's going to happen next.' Tom and I haven't been married long and I'm not sure what the trip to Thailand will bring. All I know is that I have this moment with Tom and I'm going to treasure it. I'm sure I will look back on it often over the next few weeks. Deep inside me lies the thought 'What if something happens?' 'What if this is it?' I don't dare relay these thoughts to Tom, knowing his main concern is always my safety. I don't want him to worry. So I bury the thoughts and allow our last moments together to be positive and happy.

The inescapable moment arrives. George Eliot said that 'only in the agony of parting do we look into the depths of love.' This makes sense now and as I look Tom in the eye one last time the agony is overwhelming. I have always found it very easy to depart on adventures. My independent nature has made sure of that. But now, a newly married woman, things are different. This time I'm leaving my best friend behind. I have mixed emotions of excitement, sadness and fear.

I can only imagine how the POWs felt when they left for war. They too left family, friends, girlfriends, fiancees and wives. No doubt, they were filled with mixed emotions – anticipation, fear, honour and pride. It doesn't matter what the circumstances are for having to leave a loved one, it is never easy to say goodbye.

I remind myself that Tom has been my husband for such a short amount of time and that the goodbye isn't meant to be easy. As I walk away from Tom, the tears I have held back, fall freely from my eyes. And the pain of being apart from Tom is real and at the surface.

∞ ∞

I arrive at Bangkok airport ready for an adventure. It's an exciting moment when Luke and I are reunited. We haven't seen each other since my wedding two months before. I'm filled with emotion as not only has the expedition begun, but arriving in Bangkok has brought back memories of a time in my life when I called Thailand home. During 2007-2009, I worked as a tour leader in South East Asia, and Bangkok was my base. I've spent a lot of time in this city.

Bangkok is the central hub of Asia for backpackers. If you are travelling to Cambodia, Laos or Vietnam you will most likely come to Bangkok first. Any budget backpacker who comes to Bangkok will make his or her way to Khao San Road. In my eyes it is an artificial wasteland and not a picture of the true Thailand. The road is filled with stalls selling clothing, jewellery and counterfeit DVDs and CDs. If you are in the market for a fake ID or even a university degree, then you're in the right place. There are no rules here. Even the street sellers have stopped the fun tradition of bartering, just ignoring tourists attempts at negotiation.

Khao San Road does a good job of degrading human souls. Take a walk down it at 1am and the place is filled with overcrowded bars brimming with drunk tourists dancing half naked; old white men ushering Thai girls back to their grubby hotel rooms; sleazy Thai men offering you the chance to see a 'Ping Pong Show', which has nothing to do with the game of ping pong. Instead you are coaxed into a tuk-tuk, driven to a dark street, ushered into a dingy pub, forced to pay 1000THB to then watch some poor Thai girl do things with a ping pong ball and her genitalia which you never thought possible. Khao San Road is not the Thailand I love, rather it's a place that has been created for young backpackers in search of a *good time*.

One block from Khao San Road is Soi Rambuttri, still a street designed for tourists, but relaxed, quieter and missing the creepiness of Khao San. I love to walk down this street sipping a delicious mango shake from one of the street vendors while searching out the Thai pancake man so I can sink my teeth into an oily, crunchy pancake coated in a thick layer of Nutella.

Luke and I are standing on Soi Rambuttri after a smooth trip from the airport. Things look very familiar, a few new restaurants but other than that I feel back at home immediately. After settling into our hostel we finally sit down to dinner at a street stall and begin discussing what needs to happen now that we are finally here in Thailand about to embark on this expedition.

"Well, I need to buy a few things," Luke says.

"Yeah me too. Did you get a rain poncho?" I ask, feeling nervous about the monsoonal rains we are inevitably going to encounter.

"Hmmm ... kinda, its not a very good one though. I don't think it will last the monsoonal rains if we meet them," Luke replies.

"Ok, so we need to fnd rain ponchos. I need methylated spirits for the cooker. But first thing tomorrow we need to get our maps!" I say, feeling confident that those three things will be easy to find in the next two days.

∞ ∞

Our short walk to the Thai Survey Department the following morning is interrupted constantly by Thai people stopping to give us *directions*.

"Come, come ..." a man says as he pulls me by the arm confident he knows where we are headed even though I haven't told him. Some people don't even stop they just yell from across the road, "Hello! That way!" pointing in irrelevant directions. We resist their attempts to make us deviate from our route and finally we discover the Thai Survey Department tucked away across the road from the Grand Palace. Inside the unassuming building are very official looking men in khaki green uniforms. Intimidated by them at first, we quickly discover they are extremely friendly and helpful despite their very limited English. We show them our proposed route and they get out index maps of Thailand for 1:50,000 and 1:250,000 scale maps. The man puts a line through grid boxes on the index map and says, 'Have' and 'No have', indicating which maps are available or not. The interaction is a great cultural experience. Already I feel like a true adventurer, rubbing elbows with the locals and purchasing maps that will take us deep into a land we are yet to fully appreciate. I've never felt as alive as I do when we buy a mixture of 1:50,000 and 1:250,000 maps that cover the entire route except for the final section of about 50km where there are no maps available at all. I'm anxious and excited all at the same time.

Back at our humble guesthouse we sit in our hot and stuffy room, equipped with a fan only, and pour over the maps. Due to restrictions that Thailand put on their maps being sold outside of the country, we have had to wait until our arrival to get the maps we need. Prior to this we have had Google maps which, with the satellite view, have been better than nothing. With the treasured maps now in our possession, we have three hours to do what most expeditions complete over a number of months – plan the route. Looking closely at the 1:250,000 scales maps we have for some sections we realise that this is going to be challenging. The scale of these particular maps is so big they are almost useless. Then there is the last 50km where we have no map at all. But there is nothing we can do about that. Those maps don't exist. Pencilling a rough guide of where we will start and end our days, we decide we've got a rough idea of where we are going and how long it will take. That'll have to be enough. The small details we will worry about day by day.

All we need now is a rain poncho and some methylated spirits. Thinking this is a simple task, we venture out into Bangkok to discover that it's not. We can't find either anywhere. For a country where it rains – a lot – it seems insane not to be able to find a rain poncho! Although considering Thais don't really camp, it isn't that unbelievable we can't find camping fuel for our cooker. A quick trip to Amarin Plaza and Tesco and we finally have a rain poncho and some solid fuel tablets that will have to do. It is our second day in Bangkok and with the plan to leave tomorrow we are pressed for time. We still have to pack, get Luke to teach me how to use the camera (as we will be filming the expedition) and do a blog for our website. The stress levels are high and rising every minute. Deep down I know I am not ready to leave tomorrow. I am feeling uptight and stressed. We have had no time to relax during our two days in Bangkok. I've barely even processed that I am here, let alone set my mind on what I am about to embark on.

Luke and I are walking back to our guesthouse. It's 9pm and we have just posted a blog called 'We Are Ready!' It's ironical and Luke says to me, half jokingly, "Would it be so bad if we stayed one extra day in Bangkok?"

I can't deny that I've been secretly hoping that something would stop us from starting tomorrow. The thought of postponing our departure has been planted and by the time we are back in our room we have calculated there is enough days to complete the walk if we stay in Bangkok for one extra day. It is decided. We won't leave tomorrow. The relief is overwhelming. I suddenly realise I am not coping. I am missing Tom and finding it really hard not being able to talk to him whenever I want. I ring Tom and talk over what Luke and I have decided. It feels good to cry and to get out all the fear and apprehension I have been feeling over the past two days. I realise I have lost the excitement. The fear of the unknown has taken over. The anxiety about how I'll handle the heat and the heavy backpack over the long distance has consumed me. I am exhausted – physically, emotionally and mentally. This is no way to start an expedition. The risk is we start tomorrow and then fall apart on day one and feel disheartened at our lack of progress. Or even worse, feel we can't go on. With such a large goal before us and with so much of it unknown, starting the walk emotionally drained and mentally unprepared is a recipe for potential failure.

All of this has made me appreciate even more the state the POWs were in when they arrived in Thailand to walk the 300km. Since the fall of Singapore on 15 February 1942, soldiers had been held as POWs in Changi Prison. On April 8 1943, when Japanese authorities in Changi ordered that 7000 British and Australian POWs be moved to an unknown location, the POWs had been in Changi Prison for almost a year. Lack of food had resulted in the POWs experiencing significant weight loss and illness. The POWs were told they were being moved to more comfortable camps. There would be ample food available and that they might like to bring leisure items such as a piano! If only this had been the truth.

∞ ∞

We are on the 7am river boat chugging along the dirty Bangkok river for what is starting to feel like an eternity. After a day of rest and relaxation yesterday, finally now we can say the expedition has begun. We are headed to the train station that will take us to our starting point, Ban Pong.

"We seem to have been on this boat for a long time," Luke says, confirming my unspoken fear.

"Yeah I've been thinking that as well. But I'm sure we must be coming up to Thonburi Railway stop soon ..." I reply confidently. But ten minutes later my confidence and sense of pride is long gone. I admit defeat and approach someone for help.

"Excuse me, Thonburi?" I ask the Thai lady selling tickets on the boat. She gives a blank look. "Thonburi?" I try again.

Then, "Ahhh, Thonbureeeeee!" accompanied by a long string of Thai words with exaggerated gesturing that just agitates me more.

At the next stop we are escorted off the boat by the ticket seller to another boat that is heading back in the direction we had come. We realise that though we were right on time for the river boat at 7am, we didn't know we needed to *change* boats to get to the Thonburi Railway stop. We are too late. We are miles away, trapped in a river boat and our train is departing in five minutes. We decide to head to the railway station anyway. The kind station guard at Thonburi tells us that if we take a taxi to Taling Chan Junction station we can catch the train passing by at 10am. Perfect. By the time we get to Taling Chan Junction station and sit munching on chicken sticks and sticky rice I am so sick of ... waiting! We are here, we are ready, it is time to get walking. The train is, not surprisingly, late but finally the waiting is over and we are sitting on a train destined for Ban Pong.

3

The Reality of Walking

"Everywhere is walking distance if you have the time."
Steven Wright

Ban Pong is a small town situated along the current railway line from Bangkok. The railway station is simple. On the platform a white sign has *Ban Pong* written in bold black lettering; at the entrance a small shop is selling Thai treats that are as unrecognisable as they are unappealing; and outside street vendors sell mangoes, jackfruit, rambutan and mangosteen. It's a typical picture of semi-rural Thailand. We are starting the walk here because the POWs began their 300km forced march from Ban Pong. The POWs in the F Force had arrived in Ban Pong by rail from Singapore in 1943. The journey to Thailand had been horrific. Men were placed in steel rice trucks which by day, in the sun, were like ovens and by night were freezing. Thirteen train loads of men with twenty seven men to a truck had set out from Singapore. With no room to sit or fully stand and only irregular stops for food and water, the five day journey was complete torture. Nature calls had to happen en-route inside the crowded trucks. One can only imagine the patience and tolerance this required.

Our train ride from Bangkok to Ban Pong bares no

resemblance. We sit on padded seats and watch the scenery fly by. The breeze blowing through the open windows keeps us cool. I visit the toilet on board, and as I balance myself on the raised squat toilet holding onto the grimy wall to avoid being thrown onto the urine covered floor, I know that all of this is *nothing* compared to what the POWs endured all those years ago.

Arriving in Ban Pong is a phantasmagoria of past and present. With life bustling, it is hard to imagine what it may have looked like for the POWs. In 1943 Ban Pong would have been a shabby collection of huts and shophouses but the current day Ban Pong is built up and exhibits the hustle and bustle of a modern Thai town. I suppose there would have still been Thai locals selling fresh produce and children playing in the street but amongst this whirl of life would have been 7000 walking skeletons, men who had survived a year in Changi Prison but whose bodies were now weak, frail and in some cases dying. The betrayal they must have felt when they were told they now faced a 300km march north must have torn at their spirit or what was left of it. Most of their equipment had to be left in a field, which included medical supplies and the piano they had brought. They were led down a dirt road through Ban Pong, and the local Thais followed trying to buy anything they possessed. Unfortunately their nightmare was only just beginning.

The F Force marched by night over seventeen days. The 300km was covered in fifteen stages of 20km each. They walked in pitch darkness, torrential rain, knee deep water and sometimes accidentally walked off bridges in the dark.

Luke and I have chosen to walk during the day. This will bring a different set of obstacles, mostly the sun and its relentlessness.

Raring to go, we backtrack 200m from Ban Pong Station to the junction of the railway where the line splits east to Bangkok where we have come from and north towards Kanchanaburi and further on to Nam Tok. For the first 110km we plan to follow the still existing railway line till its end in Nam Tok. It is exhilarating standing on the railway line, the place where it all began. We had not known how easy the railway line would be to follow but here we are standing on it.

"This is it!" Luke exclaims with an infectious grin on his face.

"I know I can't believe it. We are really going to do this!" I reply, smiling just as wide as my brother. For the first while, we alternate between walking on the line and on the dirt path that runs parallel. It doesn't take us long to learn just how difficult it is to hike in Thailand weather. In fact, it has only been two hours and the reality of walking has brought us to our knees.

"I need to stop," Luke mutters, collapsing to the ground. "I don't know how I'm going to do this." His face is bright red and streaked with sweat.

"Ugh!" I cry, spitting out the water I've just poured into my mouth. "The water in my bottle is boiling hot!"

The 300km before us at this moment in time seems an impossibility. Can we really succeed in doing this? Do I really want to do this? Conditions are fierce: the temperature is reaching 40°c and rising, there is 90-100% humidity and the sun's rays are burning us by the minute.

We will have to rest every half hour of walking

otherwise we are going to collapse with heat exhaustion, dehydration or fatigue. I can feel that my back is wet with perspiration and I wonder if it is seeping through to the clothes in my 20kg backpack.

We come across our first bridge. Originally there were 680+ trestle bridges along the 415km Thai-Burma railway. Not many of the originals remain today. The bridge before us is made of wood and stands twenty metres or so above the ground. Luke crosses first. I'm nervous. What if a train comes? I keep a close eye behind us. Soon it is my turn. I step onto the first sleeper. It creaks under my weight. I move forward being careful to take it slowly – one step at a time. I make the mistake of looking down between the sleepers. Big mistake. I don't like this. I feel completely vulnerable. The sleepers are old, rotting planks of wood and the creaking sounds they make remind me of a horror film sound effect. Somehow I make it to the other end alive. But this is the first bridge of many. Some will be longer, some higher and some more rickety. I'm not looking forward to any of them. In particular I'm thinking of the infamous Death Curve: the bridge at Wang Pho. I shake off the thoughts. I'll deal with that bridge when I come to it.

At dusk after trekking our first day, I'm astounded at just how tough the walking has been. We have covered about 12km today but we are going to have to do better than that. From now on we will need to cover at least 20km a day. The thought of walking those distances in this heat makes my stomach turn. But for the moment our biggest concern is where we are going to spend the night. We continue to walk down the railway line trying to spot a good place to camp. There is nowhere in sight. The railway is lined with dense shrub. I am hoping that around the bend in the distance a suitable camping site will show itself. The rumble of a motorbike tickles my ears. I realise it has stopped alongside us on the road parallel to the railway. A small Thai lady is standing up craning her neck to see us.

"Where you going?" her voice calls out across the short trees that line the railway.

"Kanchanaburi!" I yell back. It's too hard to explain our 300km walk by yelling.

"Kanchanaburi?!" she cries. She knows that is over 30km away. We must be crazy.

"Yes, well not today. We are looking for somewhere to sleep."

"Hotel?"

"Well, no, camping. Can we put our tent up at your house?" Luke asks.

"Huh?" she crinkles up her face. These *farang* are not making sense.

"Tent?" I yell.

"Huh?"

"Camping?" Luke tries.

"Huh?"

We are obviously not getting anywhere. I'm not surprised. This girl must be wondering what on earth a couple of *farang* are doing walking down the railway line at 4.30pm. Luke and I both look at each other, then turn our heads back to her and say in unison, "Can we sleep at your house?"

"My house?" she says surprised.

"Yeah," I reply, just as surprised as her that we have asked this. She looks to the sky, scrunches her nose up, chats to the guy on the bike with her then replies, "Okay."

"Are you sure?" I ask, suddenly not so sure myself of our request.

"Yes," she nods.

"Where do you live?" Luke asks.

"About 3km from here," she replies.

"Who do you live with?" I ask trying to suss out the situation we are getting ourselves into.

"My mother and my husband," she says tapping the shoulders of the man on the motorbike with her.

"Ok, so how will we get to your house?"

"We can go on motorbike. My husband will take you first." As Luke and I retrace our steps along the railway back to the road crossing where they are waiting for us, we mumble to each other. "I hope we are doing the right thing."

"At least she speaks English!" We reach the road crossing and are finally able to meet the lady properly.

"My name is Mai," she says, I grab her tiny hand to shake it, and reply, "I'm Rachel and this is Luke."

With introductions out of the way, I am first to climb onto the motorbike. Struggling to stay balanced with my big heavy backpack, Mai's husband and I drive off into the distance. I turn back to look at Luke standing on the side of the road with Mai, I hope I will see him again.

Mai's husband twists through the streets of the small town they live in. I feel free on the back of the motorbike, happy. Far in the distance the sun is setting on the horizon creating a pink haze and directly in front of me the scent of sweet shampoo is wafting up my nostrils from Mai's husband's hair. We arrive at their house. It is protected by a locked gate, and standing behind the gate is an older lady, who I assume is Mai's mother, holding a baby. Mai's husband indicates for me to get off and once I've done so, he leaves to pick up Luke. Or so I hope.

"Sawadee ka," I say to the mother.

"Sawadee ka," she replies. We then stand and stare at each other. It's a little awkward.

It is obvious this is as far as our conversation is going to go. I place my finger onto the baby's hand and he grabs on tightly. Babies are great at bringing people together. Mai's mother smiles at me. We cannot communicate with words, but we can smile and coo at the small baby in her arms. It is a special bonding moment.

I look down at my shirt. There are white salt lines all over it from all the sweating. I'm disgusting. Embarrassed I fold my arms across my chest trying to hide the salt lines. I can't even imagine what Mai's mother is thinking about me. I hope I don't have an offensive odour emitting from my pores. Soon Luke arrives. Balanced on the bike, in true Thai style, is Mai, her husband and Luke with his backpack. The Thais are amazing in what they can transport on a small motorbike. On different occasions I've seen fifty wicker chairs carefully stacked and poised; an entire family of eight strategically balanced; and a dog standing with its back paws on the seat and its front paws on the drivers shoulders.

Mai asks us to wait for ten minutes so they can get the house ready. Luke has asked Mai some questions while waiting for his lift – Mai is 28 years old, she is married and the baby is hers. She used to work in a hotel in Kanchanaburi which is why she speaks some English. I have a good feeling. I'm glad Mai stopped to talk to us. I didn't fancy a night in a tent anyway. Ten minutes later Mai resurfaces saying "Sorry for messy room. My mother not have time to make nice." We walk into a bedroom that contains a bed and air conditioning! Our first night on expedition and we have stumbled across this? I immediately feel guilty but secretly pleased.

Mai shows us the bathroom saying, "Sorry for not nice. Bathroom maybe forty years old. Sorry."

"We are not worried Mai!" I try to reassure her "This is wonderful, thank you so much."

But I feel my words are wasted. Their generosity is astonishing me but they feel their gift is too small. We exit the bedroom and enter the living room. The television is on. My head turns to look at the television screen and I am surprised by what I see. It is a wedding, a very big and elaborate one too. The bride and groom look very familiar. It is Prince William and Kate Middleton of the United Kingdom. I am looking at the Royal Wedding of the year; the wedding the world has been waiting for; the wedding that the world is stopping for. I have just walked into a room in the middle of Thailand at the moment of the wedding vows. Having lived in London during the lead up to the expedition, I have witnessed just how excited London is about this wedding. I've been a tad disappointed that I will miss out on being there during this event in history. I'd resigned myself to the fact I was not going to see the wedding but here I am, sitting with a Thai family, watching the extravagant display of western tradition.

After the ceremony Mai asks us if we want food.

In response to our 'yes', Mai's mother toddles off to the kitchen whilst Luke and I remain in the living room. The Thais love their television and our differences in culture are evident as I watch some of the quirky shows with amateur camera work and awkward television hosts. I find pleasure in observing the rest of the family fixated on the images that come from the box. I may not understand the attraction but I can relate to the joy a good television show brings.

Our dinner is soon ready and Mai's mother brings out a few plates of food. Luke and I are then left alone so we start eating. There seems to be a lot of food and we don't want to leave any for fear of offending them. We eat as much as we can. Then the rest of the family comes to sit down and Mai's mother brings out the rest of the food. Oops. I have been so used to being at *organised* home stays in South East Asia (Vietnam, Laos, Thailand, Malaysia) where my experience has been that the family doesn't eat with you. The family will generally have lost the excitement of 'getting to know the visitors' a long time ago. It hadn't even crossed my mind that we should wait. We pretend that nothing is unusual about what has happened and continue to eat with the family, despite the fact we are really full.

Thanking the family for a delicious dinner, Luke and I retire to our extravagant room. Luke removes his t-shirt to discover some serious looking sunburn on his neck. I'm concerned. It doesn't look good. At least we have discovered early that we can't underestimate the power of the sun here in Thailand.

After a much needed wash, Luke and I enjoy a sleep that is possibly a little *too* comfortable for a pair on a so called *expedition*: fluffy pillows, comfy mattress and air-conditioning.

In the morning, Mai and her husband drop us back at the railway. I'm taken first on the motorbike and left at an abandoned service station while Luke and Mai are collected by her husband. While I wait a gang of dogs emerge from the skeleton of the building. Intimidated by their presence, I stay well clear and make no eye contact. On the railway yesterday we learnt quickly that the dogs out here don't like us, don't trust us and don't want us around. They own the dirt they stand on and only God can help those who dare pass them. I study our map intently and the dogs move on making no trouble.

When Luke arrives with Mai, I try to ask if we can take a photo of all of us. She is confused by my request and I realise she is wearing her pyjamas and may not want that in the photo. Trying to calm her I say, "We can just take head shots." As I say this I make a cutting action across my throat. Mai's eyes fill with fear and she shakes her head. "Oh, no thankyou." Luke is standing behind Mai, rolling his eyes and shaking his head at me. "You're scaring her! It looks like your threatening to chop her head off," Luke says. He then explains to Mai that we want to take a photo with her and after a while Mai realises what we want and is more than happy to smile for the camera.

Just before Mai and her husband leave she suggests that we stay at temples along our journey. "It will be safer," she says. I'm curious about what danger she wants us to avoid; human or animal? We exchange email addresses and promise to let them know how we get on. Mai pleads with us, "Don't walk on railway line. Dangerous. Trains. Highway is better." As Mai rides off into the distance, Luke and I look at each other. "Do you want to walk on the highway?" Luke asks. I really don't want to. The highway is so dull to walk on and I know in the latter part of this walk we will have to be following the highway anyway. So, while the railway is here I want to stay with it. I know Luke does too. The quietness of the railway is also appealing. No trucks or cars zooming past at dangerous speeds. So despite Mai's advice, we ignore it. Her concern for us was obvious and I'm touched that she cares so much about our well-being. Mum would be so relieved knowing we had people looking out for us. That relief, though, may disintegrate if she knew we were not heeding the advice.

We head back to the railway track. Already I see the railway as a friend. Something we can rely on, put our trust in. As long as I am on that railway I feel safe, except for the trains. I'm nervous about trains bearing down on us unaware. But our new friend is not being kind today. Walking along the track is hard work and my feet are paying for it. Blisters are developing and there is not much I can do. I can't get a flat footing. The railway is strewn with millions of jagged rocks. It's not long until I'm in agony. Blisters are a walker's enemy. I stop to take my shoes off and treat the blisters. Early treatment is essential. I had been advised by another adventurer to add talcum powder and zinc tape to our first aid kit. I'm so glad I heeded that advice. My foot is drenched in sweat – but I'm able to dry out the blister with the talcum. I rip off a strip of zinc tape and place it over the blister. At least this will stop it from rubbing up against my boot.

There are so many people living along the railway. I

wonder if any of them lived here during the war? I wonder if any of them remember the POWs or the Japanese? I'm deep in thought. My thought pattern is broken by an old Thai lady waving at us calling, "Sawadee ka!" At first her wave looks more like a shooing action but then I realise its the Asiatic gesture of *come closer*. With palm facing downwards her fingers waggle backwards and forwards gesticulating that we are welcome. She then makes the universal action for drink. Luke and I turn off the track and make our way to her house. I'm excited to meet a family who lives alongside the railway line. I'm also incredibly grateful for the chance to rest. It's 11am and already the heat is stifling. Soon our hands are cooled, holding an ice cold cup of water. Not being sure where the water has come from, I pop in a chlorine tablet. Meanwhile the Thai family stands before us grinning ever so proudly! We try to communicate with each other which only results in the family giggling uncontrollably and shaking their heads in disbelief. I bet they didn't expect to meet a couple of *farang* today!

"Ban Pong?" I try to say so they will understand. The Thai language is tonal and each word can have up to five meanings or more. Ban Pong is a hard name to pronounce. I'm finding that I need to say it five or six times emphasising different parts of the word until I stumble across the right one and am eventually understood.

"Oohh, B*an* P*ong*," the elderly lady nods after a few tries. It all sounds the same to me.

"Uh, Ban Pong," I repeat, whilst gesturing with my arms and walking on the spot, "tee nee," which is Thai for *here*. With each interaction I'm learning more and more of the Thai language. Even if I can't pronounce the words right, it's exciting to be able to attempt communication with the locals in their language.

"Oohh, tee nee!" another nod of understanding. More walking on the spot, "Kanchanaburi!"

"Oohh ...!!" nods all around.

I think they have understood what we are doing. It doesn't really matter. It's nice to just be in each other's presence. I observe my surroundings. The house is a very simple, concrete style common in rural Thailand. A mango tree hovers above me, the branches hang low, heavy with sour mango, and off in the distance a man is working with his hands, creating a masterpiece. Luke and I stroll over to where he is. He is building Buddhist shrines. Now I notice them everywhere, big ones, small ones, all of them painted in many different colours. The correct names for these shrines are *spirit houses* – in Thai *San Phra Poom* – and they come in two styles: one leg and four leg. Each Buddhist household must have a spirit house. In fact, they are supposed to have more than one. This man's spirit houses are elegantly made, colourfully painted in red, blue, yellow and greens.

"Kao?" one of the ladies asks. Knowing this to mean, 'eat' in Thai, we nod. She indicates for us to enter the house. Touched by her generosity, but controlled by our own timetable, we know we can't stay. We need to get going. The heat of the day is not far off so we want to make as much distance as we can before the heat debilitates us. We try to mime the universal action for *take away*. It seems to work as the lady nods, jumps on her motorbike and rides away! I have no idea where she has gone. We sit in silence waiting for her to return.

The lady arrives back ten minutes later with food she has *bought* for us. I am taken back. How incredibly generous. She has no idea who we are. To add to the kindness she also piles our arms with bananas and sour mango from their trees. Overwhelmed, arms heavy laden with an over abundance of food, we bid the family farewell. Not far down the dirt road we have to ditch the mangoes, launching them onto a field. Unlike the sweet mango which is soft and makes taste buds sing, its relative, the sour mango is the opposite – crunchy and tasteless except for a bitter twang. They are also extremely heavy. I doubt the POWs discarded food when Thais offered it to them. I feel bad, selfish and ungrateful. But I have to remind myself we aren't here to relive the POWs experience. It's about gaining an understanding.

We are crossing another bridge. This one is really long. I'm about half way across when it starts pouring with rain. Desperate to reach the end but careful not to slip on the wet track, I quickly move forward. Safe on the other side, we decide to stop for lunch under a tree away from the rain. In the paper packages, given to us by the Thai lady, is rice and chicken. It's delicious and hits the spot. I'm so grateful for the tasty lunch. Slurping it down with pepsi and munching on a banana for dessert I smile – inside and out. I am loving this moment. This small but generous gift of lunch has stirred something within me. It's only day two but already I can sense Thai people are going to teach me something significant.

After lunch we follow the road for about an hour. Sometimes the railway is not accessible and we have to walk on the road. We must be quite a sight. White people walking, struggling under the weight of massive backpacks can't be a common occurrence out here. I notice a ute has pulled over to the side of the road, and a young Thai man is walking towards us.

"Hello! Where you going?" he asks, smiling at us.

"Um ... Kanchanaburi," Luke replies.

"Kanchanaburi! That is 30km away you know!" the man replies, shocked.

"We know, but we want to walk there." It's not easy convincing the locals that our decision isn't a crazy one.

"Kanchanaburi ... but it's far!!" the man pleads with us.

"We know but we want to walk it."

"If you want to go with me I take you almost 17km," the man looks at us, eagerly waiting our response. He seems desperate to help us out.

"No really, we want to walk."

"I'm a Tour Guide from Bangkok. I'm on my time off now. I saw you walking and wanted to help." His pristine English is explained by his role as a Tour Guide. I'm so thankful for how concerned this guy is about our well-being.

"So, will you go with me?" he pleads with us one more time. Having to break his heart again we explain that we want to walk and can't accept his offer of a lift. "No?!" he cries, "Where you from?"

"Australia," says Luke.

"Hmmm ... okay. If you have a problem, I will give you my number and you can call me."

I'm secretly relieved that we are being given a phone number of someone in Thailand. Up to this point we have had no emergency contact. The promise of assistance if we ever need it is a huge weight off my shoulders. I'm sure mum will be pleased to hear this as well.

"My name is Gene," he tells us as he recites his phone number for me to write down. "Thanks so much Gene. We will be sure to call you if we get into trouble."

"Okay, good luck!" The short encounter with Gene has really lifted my spirits. I had initially been quite scared of being out here in unknown parts of Thailand, but every day we are finding that the Thai people want to help us and will go out of their way. I'm not as scared as I was at the beginning of this expedition. It's giving me hope for the rest of our journey. .

Meeting up with the railway again we spend the remainder of the day walking through small towns, somnolent countryside and pristine rice paddy fields. As we approach Kanchanaburi, we realise we can make it there tonight but we are going to have to push ourselves.

The POWs were forced to walk 25 – 35km a night. Today is only our second day of walking. We end up walking 35km. It almost kills us. Luke's hip is in a bad way by the time we walk into town. He can barely walk. For the past three hours he has pushed on. Every twenty minutes we would stop to recuperate, bandage blisters and evaluate our situation. But pushing on has not been a wise idea. We have weeks of walking left. I can only hope rest will benefit Luke's damaged hips. We both have pushed ourselves too hard and we are completely shattered. I'm exhausted. My feet are blistered and even my hips have blisters from my backpack harness rubbing. My skin has heat rash. The heat, sun and physical strain of walking has taken its toll on us. We are not going to complete the walk if we try to cover these distances daily. At least we have learned early on that pushing your body beyond its limits in this heat can potentially kill you, or at least make you really ill. We are going to need to be careful from now on, look after our bodies.

I'm not surprised so many of the POWs died during their years on the construction of the Thai-Burma railway. In fact, I'm surprised so many of them did survive. My respect for the POWs has risen. The hardships they endured are so much more real for me now. I know this walk is going to push me to my limits and I'm scared about the 270km we still have to walk. I remind myself that anything that I endure will be nowhere near the level of suffering the POWs experienced.

We now have time to contemplate what the past two days have been like and what that means for the rest of the walk. We have arrived in a place filled with history. We are going to stay here for two nights. I want to learn as much as I can about the Death Railway and the men who worked on it. There isn't a better way to do that than in the very area where so many of the atrocities occurred, Kanchanburi.

4

Gaining an Understanding

"A warrior of light takes every opportunity to teach himself."
Paul Coelho

An overweight western man sitting at a street bar, wearing oversized USA flag novelty glasses, is calling out to us in his thick southern accent, "Welcome to Kanchanaburi! You can ride the elephants, pat the tigers, caress the ladies … now have yourself a good day!" Just one of the many characters on the tourist street of Kanchanaburi, this man hasn't left the street bar since our arrival in town the night before. I have a giggle at the idiosyncratic man but am saddened by his seemingly small world.

Kanchanaburi, as a town, has disappointed me so far. The main tourist street could be any other street on a tourist map of Thailand. It is lined with tattoo parlours, restaurants serving burgers and fries, masseurs and bars. The guesthouses offer tours to Erawan Falls, Elephant Treks, River Kwai and Hell Fire Pass – all the *must-do* attractions. I can't walk down the street without getting hassled by someone.

"Tattoo for the pretty lady?"

"Come inside please, supreme pizza very taaaaasty!"

"Thai massaaaaaaage."

"Excuse meeee, you want tour tomorrow?"

"Beer ten baaaaaht!"

The bars that line the street are covered in signs such as *'Get drunk for 10B!'* or *'Drink. Drunk. Dance.'* or *'Get shit faced on a shoestring!'* As I saunter down the street all I can think is, 'Is this what westerners are seen as by the Thai tourist industry? People who want to get drunk?!' Unfortunately, there are enough tourists coming to Thailand (and other popular tourist destinations) who do want that. Therefore, bars in Thailand's hot spots will always be offering cheap drinks. I pop my head into the bar that promises you will get drunk for 10B (equivalent 30 cents) and am crestfallen to see a group of westerners sitting together getting 'shit faced' and the men flirting with the Thai bar girls.

In contrast, surrounding the town of Kanchanaburi and in amongst these streets, there is history. History of men who died for their countries. Men who suffered for our freedom today. Atrocities that are some of the worst the world has seen, happened right where we stand. Looking at the tourists drinking heavily at the street bars, I sigh. Tomorrow many will wake up with a hangover and stumble into a minibus of a tour they have booked. They will be driven out to the famous sites; Allied War Museum, River Kwai, Hell Fire Pass. They will pay their entry fee, read the signs, and nurse their sore heads whilst taking snaps of the places they visit. For most of them that will be it. They will go home and say, 'I've visited the River Kwai.'

For what the POWs went through, one could argue that putting aside the booze for a few days together with visiting the museums would be a small sacrifice in order to show respect for those men who died and for those who still live today.

In this town the POWs of WWII endured horrific atrocities at the hands of the Japanese. It was so monstrous that it is beyond comprehension. Only if you were there could you have the ability to understand what those men experienced. Only if you were there could you share the feelings of what it was like to be tortured, starved and beaten, forced to work against your will, and to live in fear.

I wasn't there but I want to learn more about this part of history. I want to acknowledge what men, like our friend Stan, endured. I want to get a real insight into their suffering. I don't want to recreate it. I simply want to gain an understanding.

∞ ∞

Bartering with a taxi or a tuk-tuk in Thailand always comes with its inherent risks. Bartering is part of the culture in Thailand which unfortunately means so are scams on innocent tourists. Not understanding the way of negotiation, people will often pay far more than they should because, to them, it looks like a decent price. I have seen travellers into Bangkok airport pounced upon and given the ride of their life. The *ride* is that they paid 1000B for a trip that should have cost 250B. Scams like this are rife in Thailand which means you feel you can never really trust anyone. Bartering with a driver generally ends with you blissfully unaware you have been scammed or feeling like you have robbed this poor driver of his livelihood by negotiating a price from 100B to 20B. It is a tricky business, never straightforward, but it is always an adventure.

During a visit to Vietnam in 2008 I was the victim of an airport hustle in Hanoi airport. Having arrived in the country with limited understanding of their currency *Dong*, I was approached by a small Vietnamese man.

"Taxi?" he queried. Having been ripped off many times in Thailand I wanted nothing to do with him. Turning my back I simply said, "No." Problem was I had no idea where to find a taxi and I had no idea what my *Dong* converted to. The man continued to hover around me.

"Taxi?" he tried again.

"No," I said determined to figure things out myself. Travelling solo brings its challenges and arriving in a completely foreign country is one of them. The man tried again, but this time handed me his phone with an amount on it. 3000.000 it said on the screen. I had no idea what it meant. I was so confused. I had just got two million *Dong* out of the ATM machine. I looked blankly at the figure of 3000.000. I tried to do a calculation on my phone. $10AUD? The man pointed to the .000, "These are cents," he explained.

If that was the case, it was 3000 *Dong*, so I gave in. "Ok, where is the taxi?" The man came alive! Racing off at an olympic pace he made his way out of the airport and to a small white car waiting outside. Another man was at the wheel. The man jumped in the passenger seat and I got in the back. As we departed the airport I realised this was not a taxi. This was some random guy's car, and I had just got inside willingly. What an idiot. The men chatted to me with their limited English. I wasn't focusing much on the conversation as I was desperately trying to convert 3000.000 to Australian Dollars. When the reality dawned on me I felt physically ill. There were no cents in Vietnam. Just *Dong*. The decimal point had been a scam. Prying on ignorant tourists, like myself, was their game and I had fallen for it, badly. I had committed to paying these men three million *Dong*. I realised now, the equivalent of $160AUD. I could live for weeks on that amount here in Vietnam! Not to mention the fact a taxi should have cost me about $30 maximum. The men pulled over to the side of the road. My heart started beating and my palms felt cold and clammy.

"Money for petrol," the driver said.

"No," I replied firmly.

"Money for toll," the driver tried.

"No, I'm going to be paying you enough money when you drop me off," I said, refusing to fall for any more scams.

Though calm on the outside, inside I was falling apart. What were these men going to do to me! I'd just refused to give them money. The driver turned and continued to drive. Thankfully on arrival at the toll he paid it himself. It was a long, nerve wracking drive into Hanoi city. When it came time to get out of the taxi I decided to play dumb. I handed over 3000 *Dong*.

"Noooooo ..." the men cried.

"What?!" I cried back.

Pulling at my wallet the man took a 100000 *Dong* note out and put the figure 30 into his phone. I didn't even have that much money on me.

"No have," I said.

"No worry, ATM," the driver replied. The men drove

me around town looking for an ATM. I was terrified. Not wanting to upset them I went along with it all. Retrieved more money from the ATM and gave what we had 'agreed' and I was left with 20000 Dong. Then the guy had the nerve to put his fingers to his mouth and say, "Hungry ..."

"No way!" I yelled, "I've given you enough money already!" I jumped out of the car and walked away not turning back, kicking myself for being so stupid and allowing myself to be scammed. In hindsight I was also thankful that nothing dangerous happened. Needless to say, these days I struggle to trust any taxi or tuk-tuk driver in South East Asia.

∞ ∞

Luke and I have just bartered with a wrinkly old Thai man to take us out to the JEATH War Museum. Fifty *Baht* is the price we have negotiated and when the ride takes half an hour I know 50B was a fair amount. Yesterday we paid 80B for a ten minute tuk-tuk ride. What a rip off that was! But nothing compared to the Vietnam ordeal, so I sit back in silence and enjoy the ride.

The JEATH War Museum (JEATH = Japan, England, America, Australia, Thailand, Holland) is housed in a replica long house on the outskirts of Kanchanaburi. Long houses are what the POWs stayed in during the war. It is a tiny museum mainly consisting of fading photos, POW paintings and artefacts from the war. It is Thai managed which means it is a little run down but incredibly authentic. While Luke is busy filming some establishing shots for the documentary, my eyes are transfixed on a statue of a Japanese soldier, Takashi

Nagase, born in Okayana City, Japan in 1918. The army sent him to Thailand as an interpreter but it is his life after the war that gets interesting. When WWII finished, Takashi had a change of heart about the Japanese actions during the war. He returned to Thailand to aid in the search for graves of lost POWs who had passed away on the line. Takashi devoted himself to society and became an ordained Buddhist monk. He established the River Kwai Peace Foundation which has given thousands of scholarships to poor students in Kanchanaburi. It's an inspiring story and it has roused something within me – the promise of hope. There is always hope; hope for change, hope for a better future. I've enjoyed the quick visit to the JEATH War Museum but we have so much more to see. So it's back in the tuk-tuk and we head to the Allied War Cemetery.

The Allied War Cemetery holds the graves of men from Australia, Britain and Holland. It is a beautifully kept garden with gravestones standing in straight regimental lines. It is a peaceful place and a feeling of hope lingers in the air. Many ex-POWs visit Kanchanaburi every year. Our tuk-tuk driver tells us of an elderly Australian man he picks up from Bangkok airport in his taxi each year. One year the Thai man asked him, "Why you come so far to Thailand and not see other places? Every year you come here to Kanchanaburi. Why?"

The elderly man simply replied, "I come to spend time with my friends."

That explains this place perfectly. The Allied War Cemetery is a space for those who died, to rest. It is also a space for those who survived, to spend time with their friends. I feel honoured to be able to visit such a blessed site.

Luke is setting up the camera so we can film video diaries. The backdrop of the cemetery seems a fitting scene. It's taking Luke a long time. I'm quickly learning to appreciate the work and time that goes into documentary making. I sit in shot so he can test the lighting and focus and lots of other technical things I do not understand. The sun's rays are beating down on me, sweat is pouring down my face and I'm trying to remain patient.

Just as Luke says, "Ok, I'm ready. Do you know what you're going to say?" the skies open. Torrential rain is now teeming down on us. "RUN!" Luke screams through the large drops threatening his camera equipment. We bolt to a shelter on the other end of the cemetery. It's a struggle. Luke flings his thongs off to make for easier running and my pants are falling off my waist because they are too big. We make it to the shelter and wait for the rain to die down.

This is the first rain we have experienced. The monsoon rain phenomenon only lasts for short periods but brings more water than you ever thought possible. I'm glad that, for the moment, we are sheltered. But now having seen the rain, I'm not looking forward to future days when we will be out there in it with nowhere to hide. Soon the rain dies down and we are left with increased humidity. The air is heavy with water and the entire cemetery is sauna steamy. We film our video diaries sharing our thoughts so far. Finally we can go. I'm so glad to leave the cemetery as the humidity, the steaminess and the heat is suffocating. We cross the road and enter the air conditioned Thai Burma Railway Centre.

This is a fantastic museum. With nine informative galleries, it really helps to create a sense of the Death Railway. Walking into Gallery One, we enter a replica of a carriage that the POWs were transported in from Singapore. Even standing inside this carriage I still can't imagine squatting for five days with twenty seven other people. As I read the signs, I'm surprised how much I already know. I guess all my reading in preparation for the trip has paid off. The signs explain about the Japanese expansion into Asia and the Pacific, and how the Japanese transported POWs throughout its new empire. It explains that Japan needed to find a safe land route to newly invaded Burma. That route would become known as the Thai-Burma Railway.

Gallery Two is all about the design and construction of the railway. What strikes me most in this gallery is the artefacts from the railway recovered from the jungle, such as huge nails bigger than a man's finger. I'm fascinated that over sixty years ago men were working with these very nails, hammering them into the sleepers of the railway. Now I'm looking at the rotting remnants in a museum.

Gallery Three explains the geography and route of the railway with a 3D model. The model also has the locations of the POW camps which can be illuminated by the press of a button. I press the Wang Pho button, a small light shines not far from where the Kanchanaburi light is. Soon Luke and I will be in Wang Pho. I shudder at the reminder of the Death Curve with its bridge that hugs the cliff line, hundreds of metres above the jungle floor. Pressing the Konkuita button, I see the light has lit up right in the centre of the large dam that was built in the 1980's. The dam covers an enormous section of the railway line. Looking at this 3D map is reminding me just how far we have to walk. The mountainous terrain is evident on the 3D map and it makes me nervous. The mountains loom above the land and I can't imagine what their presence will feel like out on the road.

Gallery Four is describing what life was like in the POW camps. The terrible conditions, inadequate food and increasing deaths. There is a quote from the diary of an F Force POW, Eric Stone — "Leave at night. Weather terrible. Track nothing but mud. Cannot see. Boys tired. This is murder. Help one another along." It's a humbling yet eerie feeling reading the words of a POW who walked the infamous F Force march.

Many factors contributed to the chances of survival for a POW. These included whether a camp was in a healthy location, had a good clean water supply, access to food supplies, or was close to the railway construction site. A summary of the death count from July 1942 – October 1943 shows that as time went on, things only got worse.

Year	Country	Deaths
July 1942–Feb 1943	USA	0
	Dutch	136
	Australian	27
	British	255
Mar – May 1943	USA	4

	Dutch	118
	Australian	148
	British	430
June – Oct 1943	USA	88
	Dutch	1303
	Australian	1630
	British	4283

With every step, every sign, every fact, every number – I'm learning. I'm understanding that this is so much bigger than me, and our walk. These men suffered, lived through hell and so many of them continue to suffer and live through hell today.

I enter Gallery Five and am shocked by what I see. It is a graphic life size hospital which displays an amputation surgery and ulcer patient undergoing treatment. It's revealing, eye opening but, most of all, disturbing. With no supplies and limited resources, the doctors had to make-do with what they had or could obtain. This resulted in water containers, artificial legs, instrument containers and bed pans all made out of bamboo. I'm almost brought to tears when I read a quote from Major A E Saggers 2nd in command of Malay Hamlet,

"Men taken from hospital were lined up with
others, many would break down and cry, others
would vomit while others would defecate from

nervousness and or illness. Others stayed in the mud in the ranks awaiting the order to move, pitifully conserving their strength. The faces of all appeared haggard and drawn and it was perfectly apparent that all were suffering from extreme exhaustion and undernourishment."

Tears flow as I enter Gallery Six where a plank of wood representing each country displays the summary of deaths represented by a nail. One nail equals five hundred deaths. There are too many nails in those planks of wood.

The next three galleries talk about the railway in operation, the bombing of the railway by the WWII Smart Bomb and also about what's happened since the war including, searching for graves of POWs lost.

The creator of the Thai Burma Railway Centre is Rod Beattie. Rod is the man we contacted right at the start of this expedition when we were trying to come up with our 'idea'. We are keen to meet him but the likelihood of that isn't high. We haven't seen an office where he might reside and he might not even be here seeing as he spends a lot of his time out in the jungle. But I'm hopeful, and when we enter the cafe that overlooks the Allied War Cemetery I see a confident looking man speaking with two Japanese people supporting some hefty video equipment. It has to be him. Luke and I cash in our *Free Tea or Coffee* tickets we got when we paid the admission, and wait. I'm trying to be discreet but I'm also keeping my eye on the man. I don't want to miss the chance to say hello to him.

About fifteen minutes later everyone at their table stands up. The man comes over to pay his bill. We just happen to be right near the counter.

"Hi, are you Rod?" I ask.

"Yes I am," Rod replies.

"I'm Rachel and this is Luke. I actually emailed you about nine months ago about walking the Death Railway," I say, hoping he will remember me. To my surprise, despite the passage of time and his busy life he says, "Oh yes, I remember you," he replies.

"Well we are here and we are two days in!" Luke says.

Rod is very encouraging but also brutally honest. When I say it has been tough so far he just laughs and says, "Wait until you get further north, those mountains are big and that will be your real challenge!" His words are making me really, really nervous. To be honest, I haven't given much thought to the mountains. I've been taking this expedition a moment at a time from the beginning. But after the first two days of walking and Rod's words, I'm now terrified. We ask Rod if it's possible to follow the railway line all the way to Nam Tok. "I don't see any problem with walking directly on the railway line. In fact, I often do it when I'm out there. I get some funny looks from the locals but it's good fun! Yeah, you could walk all the way to Nam Tok if you like."

Rod has to get going. He is filming with a Japanese film crew today. It's really great to see Japan embracing this part of history. It's been interesting meeting Rod. I leave the museum feeling quite solemn. I have a lot on my mind. The days ahead are not going to be easy.

Luke and I have one more place to visit. It's the

WWII Museum. The Lonely Planet guide doesn't talk this place up at all, stating it is 'kitschy and touristy'. Therefore, I don't have high expectations. But the WWII Museum surprises me. For a while we can't find anything of interest, just levels and levels of Thai art. However, when we venture into the basement we find a treasure. The museum is filled with hundreds of items the Japanese abandoned in the jungle at the end of the war. There are cars, hundreds of motorbikes, train carriages, weapons and so much more. I feel like I've been allowed into the enemy's home. Being amongst these relics is changing the way I look at this expedition. I feel more connected to it. Now when I try and imagine the Japanese, I can picture the car I'm currently standing in front of. I find a piece of Japanese uniform displayed. The sign on it says, 'Japanese man who wishes to remain nameless returned this piece of clothing to Thailand to regain peace and healing.' A small gesture that says a lot.

Our two days in Kanchanaburi have opened my eyes. I have gained a much greater understanding of the war that was fought here and the atrocities that were faced. I don't want us to re-create what the POWs experienced. That was never our plan. It would be offensive to even try. Their forced march was a walk from hell to hell. Our walk is done by choice, in honour of the POWs. Our walk is no comparison. They are two separate things.

5

Norn Lup?

*"They dressed in bright orange robes, and had shaved heads
and golden skin. Every morning before dawn,
they streamed out of the temples in long lines,
alms bowls in hand, collecting their daily food from
the townspeople, who would kneel in the streets to
offer up rice for the monks."*
Elizabeth Gilbert (Committed)

It is so much smaller than I expected. Before me stands
the Bridge Over the River Kwai, as it has become famously
known. I'd envisaged a much larger structure but this is tiny. It
almost looks like a toy. It is striking though. The outline of the
bridge against the sun rising in the east depicts an aura of
strength. The bridge holds memories of pain, heartache and
loneliness. It's an important part of history because for us it
now symbolises strength, endurance and hope. Ironically, this
bridge was originally built out of wood by the POWs but soon
bombed and destroyed. The steel bridge was in fact brought
over from Java in sections. Once constructed, this bridge was
also bombed. The bridge that crosses the river today was
repaired after the war.

Such an iconic symbol of the Thai-Burma Railway, it is

essential Luke gets some shots of this for the documentary. As I wait for him to do his thing, I sit down so as to conserve my much needed energy. I have no idea what is ahead of us. It is incredibly exciting and almost overwhelmingly scary. We are about to cross the bridge over the River Kwai and just keep walking. I feel like the adventurer I've always wanted to be, testing the limits society places on us, by going beyond the norm and risking our well-being and safety by stepping into the unknown.

It's time to go. Luke and I casually stroll across the bridge. It's far too early for any tourists to be out and about. We have the bridge to ourselves this morning except for a couple of fisherman who have cast their nets over the side. They have a decent amount of fish already in their bucket. We stop to say hello. Just as we do I hear a loud horn. It's a train. We stand up against the railing and watch the train chug past us. It's slightly intimidating being so close to the great machine. Large brown eyes are peering down at us like puppies staring out a car window. All the eyes belong to Thai locals. Once again, it's far too early for any tourist to be out and about.

The heat is already debilitating. It's unbelievable. We are in for an incredibly hot day. Luke is carrying five kilograms of camera equipment on this trip. An extra burden for him. In preparation he designed a camera bag that he could carry in front of him attached to the straps of his backpack. The problem is it does not give easy access to the camera. When he comes across something he wants to shoot, he has to set up the camera with microphone and sound box. It all takes about two to three minutes. This is precious time that cannot be wasted when it comes to filming. So Luke has been carrying the camera by the strap on his shoulder. It's an obvious strain and irritant on his body, especially his bad back. As we cross the bridge I notice Luke has rested the camera in the open camera bag. It looks precariously balanced.

"Is that how you are going to carry the camera?" I ask.

"Yeah, it'll be okay. If I trip I'll be able to grab it," Luke replies. I think he is taking a big risk, but I don't say anything. I know how much he is beginning to hate carrying that camera and I'm also too tired and hot to object. I'll worry about it later, I think to myself.

As we continue walking I turn and realise the bridge is no longer in sight, lost beyond the curve in the line. Ahead of us is farm land and mountains lining the horizon. It is stunning, but the spectacle of it all is masked by the heat of the day. There is no shade. No escaping the sun. It's unbearable. To make matters worse, the line here is also strewn with those damn rocks. My blisters are irritated and starting to throb.

We walk for a good few hours, stopping every fifteen minutes for a rest and drinking more water than I ever thought possible. At one of our many rests, I notice a concrete gutter about fifty metres off the left side of the track. It's about one metre deep and it is covered by trees. Shade – we can't resist. I jump down into the gutter to search for a good place to sit.

"Watch out for the ants," Luke says.

Suddenly I hear a loud thump and sickening crack. I turn to find Luke's camera lying at the bottom of the concrete gutter. My heart sinks and my stomach turns inside out.

"Oh no ..." I say as I pick up the camera. I can't bear to look at Luke. This equipment has cost him thousands and thousands of dollars. Nothing good can come of this. As I take a peak at the lens I cringe in horror – there is a definite fracture in the glass. I hand it to Luke who takes a look at it. Thankfully the lens itself is not broken, which is amazing after the tumble it took, but the filter is cracked.

"Does it matter?" I ask.

"Well, it means I can't take arty shots. It means I can't do a lot of what I have been doing. It's gonna have a big effect on the documentary. Basically, this is really depressing."

I don't know what to say. We are in the middle of nowhere and Bangkok is a *long* way away. There is no hope of getting this repaired. I know what I want to say. I want to be the big nagging sister who says, "I told you so. I knew you shouldn't be carrying it like that." But of course I don't say that because in moments like these, it doesn't matter anymore what you should have done or said. It's happened. I have never wanted to turn back time as much as I do right now. Wanting Luke to have as much time as he needs to process this, I remain silent and wait. Luke sits on the gutter edge with his head in his hands. Every so often he picks up the camera to test a few things or simply stares at the crack in the filter.

"It's so depressing," I hear him mutter quite a few times. It's such an awful moment.

"I was worried about the ants!" Luke remembers. "I was too tired, too hot and I forgot I had it sitting like that. This is what happens in these extreme conditions. You get lazy and things don't get done properly," Luke sighs.

"Mmmm ..." I manage to get out, I have no idea how to console this poor guy. Words have escaped me.

"It wouldn't have mattered so much if we were near

the end of the trip, but we are only days in! It sucks man."

I can't believe he isn't crying. I know if it were me and my dream had been tainted by my own actions, I would be in tears. Maybe that is why I'm finding it so hard to know what to do. Luke is so silent, so solemn – I can't read any of it. A train passes and I can see curious tourists peering out the window at us as they chug slowly down the railway track. I can just imagine the conversations people are having, 'Look! There are two white people over there?' I feel so far away from those tourists in every way; distance, lifestyle, dreams and reality. Seeing the train is a reminder that though we might feel we are in the middle of nowhere, civilisation isn't too far away at the moment. Yet the further we walk the more isolated we will become. Soon the signs will no longer be in English and we will be relying fully on our maps, our instincts and assistance from the local people. Eventually Luke says he is ready to go. He puts the camera back resting in the camera bag but this time he puts the strap of the camera around his neck.

"This was all I needed to do. This would have stopped the camera falling," Luke says. Hindsight is a wonderful thing, but sometimes it's a slap in the face. We get up and do that thing we came to do – walk.

It's closing in on midday. Time for lunch. Every part of my body is crying for shade, some relief from the sun. We step off the line and find a tree to sit under. It's not comfortable and there is no breeze but it will have to do.

Luke makes an interesting observation, "About this time each day I've noticed that the breeze disappears. There is no movement in the air." It explains why we crash at this time each day. The lack of movement in the air creates an atmosphere of despair. I can't move. I have no motivation to get up let alone walk. We sit and eat our lunch, mostly in silence.

After a good two hours of rest Luke makes another observation, "Look, I've tied a piece of string around the filter which is stopping it from moving. Then if I place the filter so that the crack is at the bottom of the shot, you can't see the crack!" I take a look at the camera screen. He is right! There is no sign of the crack. It is hidden.

"Awesome, so you can still use it?"

"Looks like, I'll just have to be really careful. It's fragile and that crack could get bigger." It's good news and on that note we decide to keep moving.

∞ ∞

"So we should try and sleep at a wat tonight, yeah?" I ask Luke.

"Yeah, for sure," Luke eagerly replies.

We have just entered the town of Wang Yen. It's not very big but we know there is a temple here, somewhere. Standing at a T-junction, we are debating which way to go when a *songtheow* (a Thai ute with seats in the tray and an awning) pulls up beside us. To my surprise a monk is sitting in the passenger seat peering out at us. "Sawadee kup!" the monk says as he winds down his window. "Sawadee ka!" I reply.

"Are you ok?" he asks.

"We are looking for the wat?" Luke tells the monk.

"Wat?"

"Wat ..."

"Wat?"

"What?"

The monk frowns. So do I. What? "We are looking for the temple?" Luke tries.

"Ooohh, the temple. The wat!"

That's what we said.

"Yes!" I cry in relief.

"Oh, very far!" he replies. That can't be right, because we know there is one around here and it has to be close. Luke whispers to me, "I think he is talking about a tourist temple that I saw a sign for before. It was about 35km away."

"Oh great, how are we going to communicate this to him," I say to Luke. The monk is now out of the car and staring at our maps. There is more confused dialogue with directions that are not of any help to us. I finally decide to try and explain, "We want to sleep at the temple, at the wat?"

"Slip?"

"Um no, sleeeeep," I enunciate. It doesn't help.

"Where is the Thai phrase book?" Luke asks.

"Good idea." I pull it out of my bag and search for the word sleep. Handing it to the monk he takes one look and then says, "You want to sleep at temple?"

"Yes!" Luke and I cry in unison. Finally we have communicated with this lovely man.

"Ok! Come ..." he ushers us into the back of his songtheow and off we go! It's a short five minute drive to the local temple, Wat Na Kan. The ute pulls over and the monk gets out of the vehicle.

"Please have some fruit."

He hands us a bag of sour mango. I'm grateful, but won't be eating them in a hurry. The man is so pleased to have been able to assist us.

"Kop kun ka," I thank him. The monk and his driver leave us at the gate of the temple. I'm not sure where they are going, but assume he must not be from this wat.

We wander onto the grounds of Wat Na Kan. Being the first temple we have approached, we have no idea how to go about asking to sleep at a wat. Orange robes hanging to dry stand out against the chocolate wood of some cabins. It must be the monks quarters. So we sidle up to the stairs and find a monk and some young boys who are very surprised to see us.

"Sawadee ka ... um, we want to sleep at the wat?" I say slowly, articulating the words and putting my hands in the sleep position.

The monk jumps up and indicates for us to follow him. Wow! I didn't think it would be this easy! We follow the monk as he jumps some stairs two at a time towards some construction men working on a section of the temple. The monk starts conversing with the construction men while the temple boys come over to us juggling a tray with glasses and jug of water. I notice the monk is now on a mobile phone. Firstly, monks have mobile phones? Secondly, who is he calling? Fifteen minutes later we are still sitting there clueless as to what is going on. The monk hands Luke the phone. Luke looks blankly as he listens to the person on the other end.

"What are they saying?" I ask. Luke hands me the phone. All I can hear is a man saying, "Where you go?"

When I reply, "We would like to sleep at the wat," there is complete silence. I can hear the tumble weed rolling by. It is now apparent that no one understands us, knows what we want or why we are here. I decide it's time for the phrase book again. I find the word for sleep – norn lup. The temple boys notice the book and come to hover over my shoulder.

"Norn lup?" I say to one of the boys. His eyes light up and he nods like crazy.

"Norn lup, norn lup!" he repeats. They understand! The temple boys drag us by the hand and usher us into a room. They quickly get to work, sweeping and bringing in mats, pillows and best of all, a fan.

The cabin where we have been placed is obviously the monks' quarters. It's just one big platform raised about ten metres from the jungle floor with rooms on one side. I notice a man in a yellow shirt coming up the stairs. He approaches us and says in very good English, "Hello, what is it you require?"

"We would like to sleep at the temple."

"You would like to sleep at the temple?"

"Yes, we are doing a very long walk."

"A long walk?"

"Yes, we are walking from Kanchanaburi to Sangkhla Buri."

"Sangkhla Buri? That is very far!"

"Yes, we know. It's about 300km!"

"Why are you doing this walk?"

"We are walking in memory of prisoners of war from WWII that were forced to build the Death Railway. I guess you could say we are doing a pilgrimage."

"Oh, ok. So you are doing a pilgrimage. And you would like to sleep at the temple."

"Yes."

"Do you require any assistance from the monks?"

"No, all we want is a place to sleep."

Patrick, we discover, is a local man who speaks English from the town of Wang Yen. It seems the monks contacted anyone and everyone who spoke English in Wang Yen. Patrick was the one who responded to the call. Patrick has relayed this information to the monks and all is settled. The monks know why we are here and are happy for us to stay.

Patrick says, "The monks want to know if you would like to come to afternoon prayers?"

"Sure. When will it be?" Patrick turns to ask the monks. "Oh, it's now!" he replies, surprising himself.

We enter the temple with Patrick to find a spectacular scene. Covering the ceiling are the branches of an imitation Bodhi tree.

The Buddha found enlightenment under a Bodhi tree in India. According to Buddhist texts, Buddha spent a whole week in front of the tree after enlightenment, staring at it with unblinking eyes. My eyes are also getting dry looking at the tree. The heart shaped leaves stretch across the ceiling and in the centre of the room is the trunk. Thick and majestic, peace permeates the atmosphere surrounding it.

The monks are kneeling at the altar which has statues of various Buddha. I smile when I notice they are using a laptop to accompany their chants – these are modern monks with mobiles and laptops! We kneel at the back and watch as they carry out their prayers. It is mesmerising; the chanting, the humming and the melodic murmurs fill the temple and my inner being.

Patrick mentions that every Buddhist man in Thailand

should, at some point in his life, go to the temple to be a monk. Some men will be at the temple for a few weeks, months or years; others dedicate the rest of their lives to monkhood.

The monks at Wat Na Kan have invited us to join them in the morning for their collection of alms. The collection of alms is a time for lay Buddhists to give respect to Buddhist monks. Each morning a monk will go on a daily alms round to collect food. The monk, wearing no shoes, will follow the same four kilometre route every day. Often a monk will have temple boys who join him. The job of the temple boy is to help the monk carry the food he collects. Patrick informs us he will join us in the morning as well. It seems the monks are nervous because they can't communicate with us in English. Having Patrick with us will be a comfort for us all. I discover that Patrick is actually from Hong Kong but is married to a Thai woman. It will be his introduction to the collection of alms as well!

The temple boys have grabbed my hand and are pulling me to a row of doors underneath the temple. Behind these doors are bathrooms consisting of a squat toilet and a gigantic tub of water for bathing. Luke and I grab our stuff and enjoy an extremely refreshing bucket bath. As I wash I'm mesmerised by the bottles of shampoo and tubes of toothpaste that belong to the monks. I'm inside the life of a monk. I never thought shampoo would intrigue me so much. I've also never appreciated a wash as much as I do on this expedition. Just to be able to get rid of all the salt off my skin makes a world of difference to how I feel.

∞ ∞

Sleeping like the monks on the wooden floor, the roosters decide to wake us up very early. Luke is less than impressed at the 3am wake up call. At 5.30am we can hear the monks shuffling around in their rooms preparing themselves for the morning's alms round. I peek out the window of our room. It is still dark but I can see the silhouette of Patrick on the road. At 6am we all set off down the road walking in a line: monk, three temple boys, Patrick, Luke and myself. The sun is just rising as we leave the temple and walk through the countryside. Passing farmland, the sun's rays glisten on the dew resting on the tapioca leaves. The temperature is perfect. If only the rest of the day could be so cool and refreshing. I now understand why the monks do this so early; to escape the heat. Along the road, as we pass houses, the monk approaches locals who are waiting for him. The local puts rice in the monk's alms bowl and the temple boys take any other food (chicken, cabbage, omelette etc) and place it in extra canisters they carry. The local then kneels, taking the prayer position for a blessing from the monk.

Just as the soft rains fill the streams,

pour into the rivers and join together in the oceans,

so may the power of every moment of your goodness

flow forth to awaken and heal all beings.

Those here now, those gone before, those yet to come.

By the power of every moment of your goodness

May your heart's wishes be soon fulfilled

as completely shining as the bright full moon,

as magically as by a wish-fulfilling gem.

By the power of every moment of your goodness.

May all dangers be averted and all disease be gone.

May no obstacle come across your way.

May you enjoy fulfillment and long life.

For all in whose heart dwells respect,

who follow the wisdom and compassion, of the Way

May your life prosper in the four blessings of old age, beauty,

happiness and strength.

The blessing is sung, in Thai, in the archetypal melodious singing voice of monks. It is enchanting. Each person who gives, receives a blessing. I can sense how important these blessings are to those who receive them. As we continue on our morning walk the monk strolls along, head posed perfectly, as though he was in another world. A world where everything is okay, where life is simple and free. I'm quietly jealous.

On arrival back at the wat, Patrick says the monks have invited us to have breakfast. "Monks cannot eat in the presence of others. So we will eat after them," Patrick informs us.

"What happens when they return from collection of alms?" I ask.

"They sort through the food. Food is then offered to the Buddha statues. They then do some chants. Only then can they eat," Patrick explains.

It's already 8.30am but we can't decline this offer. What an experience it has been so far. I can't quite believe it is all happening. While we wait, Patrick tells us of a conversation he had with his wife last night, "I told my wife last night that there were two foreigners planning to walk from Ban Pong all the way to Sangkhla Buri. She has advised me that this is very dangerous, it is not safe for the foreigner to walk there. Walking to Nam Tok is okay but from there I think it is better that you catch a bus to Sangkhla Buri. There are Burmese tribes, the Mon and Karen, in the north near the border. It is too dangerous for you to be walking in those areas."

His words make me nervous but I know we won't be changing our plans. We make no promises but instead thank him for his advice.

Soon it is time for us to eat. The monks have finished and immediately go about their daily chores. Luke and I enter the room to find the temple boys arranging plates and the left over food on the floor. They indicate for us to sit down. Patrick, the temple boys, the workmen, Luke and I tuck straight into the food. There are twenty five dishes in total; chicken, cabbage, chilli pork, and my favourite bamboo shoot curry. Of course there is also rice, a lot of rice. I look around at all the people we are sharing a meal with. What an absolute privilege this is.

Our first stay at a temple has been an incredibly positive one. We have been welcomed, fed and housed. The monks have been so friendly. We have also really enjoyed spending time with Patrick our temporary translator. While Luke and I are packing our bags, I notice Patrick walking towards his four wheel drive. It seems Patrick is leaving without saying goodbye. The differences in culture are evident in times like this. I'm disappointed not to be able to say goodbye or thankyou to anyone. The monks have vanished too. Our spontaneous visit to Wat Na Kan has been eye opening, inspiring and a highlight of our adventure so far. It's 9am and the temperature has risen dramatically already. We are in for a hot day of walking, but I don't care. It's been worth it.

6

Backpacks Buddhist Temple Sanctuary

"Let us rise up and be thankful,
for if we didn't learn a lot today, at least we learned a little,
and if we didn't learn a little, at least we didn't get sick,
and if we got sick, at least we didn't die; so,
let us all be thankful."
Siddhartha Buddha

I am trudging along behind Luke who is about twenty metres ahead of me. Usually we walk together but today the heat is too much. I can't keep up. I've also got a lot on my mind. I can't stop thinking about Patrick's words, "It's not safe for the foreigner to walk to Sangkhla Buri." Are we doing the right thing? Are we walking into a perilous land of volatile tribal people who can't be trusted? What have I got myself into?

The Karen people are the largest of over twenty minority groups that have fought the Burmese government. Apparently, as recently as last year, the Burmese Army was burning down Karen villages displacing thousands of people. Over 200,000 Karen people were driven from their homes during the decades of war in Burma with most of the refugees in Thailand being from the Karen tribe. The Mon tribe has also risen in revolt against the Burmese government. I can't imagine the lives that these people live. They would be encountering conflict on a daily basis. I hope we don't find ourselves immersed in any of this daily warfare.

I look up and notice a cyclist powering towards us. I figure this has to be a westerner as I haven't seen any avid Thai cyclists around. I'm right and as he passes us the man waves, slows down and turns back to where we are standing.

"Hello there! What are you two up to?" he asks as he takes a big swig of water from his bottle.

"We are walking to Ban Kao," I reply, choosing to give our destination for the day to avoid the look of confusion we are getting used to. However, I'm the one surprised when he replies, " Ah right, so you're walking to Ban Kao onto Sai Yok and all the way to Sangkhla Buri?"

"Yes! That's exactly what we are doing!" Luke and I cry in unison. I'm dumbfounded. Everyone we have met so far has been open about how ridiculous they think our walk is. Here is someone who not only agrees with us, but has guessed what our goal is.

"That's fantastic! Only way to do it I reckon, except for on a bike of course," he replies grinning. "You're from England are you?" he says looking at me. I get this a lot. Having lived in the UK for two years, I've adapted to my surroundings more than I'd have preferred.

"No, Australia, although I live in the UK so maybe I've picked up some of the accent."

"Ah well," he said, "I'm originally from England but

have lived in Australia and Thailand so we are all a bit of it ain't we." I couldn't agree more and am enthralled by this man standing before me. Walking day after day, with only your brother for company, the sight of another westerner who seems to *get* what you are doing is a big morale lifter.

"I cycle all round these parts, all the way up the highway through Burma and along the border. All the border police guards know me and want me to have a drink with them all the time," he boasts. "These parts are beautiful, I live just back near the town. I got myself a small farm where I built a beautiful Spanish style house, three bathrooms and bedrooms. I have a gate and I lock it at night. I tell them all, 'I got a gun so you try anything, I'll get ya!'"

I smile realising I am talking to quite a character – one of the many *westerner retirees* who moves to Thailand for the cheap living and warm conditions.

"I cycle fifty to one hundred kilometres a day, swim four kilometres each morning. I'm seventy years old!"

For the second time in the past five minutes, I am shocked. This guy is seventy! Now I look closer at his face. I can see his skin is leathery, wrinkly and tanned but this man is incredible. His life of daily exercise makes him look like he could run up Mount Everest and not break a sweat!

"Each birthday I get my partner on the motorbike and I hold on and do seventy miles an hour. Next birthday it'll be eighty, but I'm not sure what I'll do for ninety or one hundred?! Maybe make it kilometres instead!" he laughs causing his eyes to disappear into his wrinkles. There is no doubt that this guy is an adventurer at heart and must have a lifetime of stories.

"My house cost £10,000 to build. Can you believe it?"

No, I can't believe it. Everything this guy says is making me want to move permanently to Thailand.

"If I'm warm, I'm happy. I went back to England at Christmas and it was bloody awful! Minus seventeen degrees it was! I was all rugged up and I was bloody miserable!" he cries.

I nod profusely knowing exactly what he means. I've spent two winters in the UK and have been miserable for most of the seven months of the bitterly cold, drab weather.

"Well, I better get cycling again. It was lovely to meet you both. My name is Barry."

"I'm Luke and this is Rachel," Luke says.

"Good luck with your walk!" he says, "Oh, and don't trust the Thai's too much ok, mostly they are fine. It's just common sense stuff really," Barry adds with a wink. Before cycling off he also warns us, "You gotta watch out for the Burmese because they are here illegally you know. They can't work. Anyway, all the best! Nice to meet you."

Barry cycles off into the distance and out of our lives. But he has left a huge impact on me. We meet so many people during the day and most of them think we are crazy walking soo far! It has been encouraging to meet someone who not only thinks what we are doing is great, but encourages us to keep going. I can't help but ponder on his words, " You gotta watch out for the Burmese ..." I don't know what to believe anymore. It feels like every person we meet has his own opinion on the odds of our successfully and safely completing this walk. I'm learning that sometimes you just have to listen to your heart and trust your own instincts. Some suggestions I take; some I leave.

Owing to our late start, the temperature is killing us.

When we stop off at a road stall to buy some drinks, I notice they have a sprinkler on out the front. I take my pack off and stand in the spray of the sprinkler. Suddenly the spray disappears! The stall owner has turned it off. Jumping up and down, I ask her to turn it back on. Crazy *farang*! She may think I'm crazy but that water has made all the difference. About three minutes later though it has all evaporated off me and I'm back to being dry, hot and bothered.

A van pulls over and a man yells out to us, "Where you going?" I'm getting used to this. Today our destination is Ban Kao so that is what we tell him. "Ban Kao," I yell back. The driver indicates for us to get in the back of his ute.

"No, we walk!" Luke tells him.

"Walk?" the man yells back. There is that usual look of shock and surprise.

"Yes, walk!" I yell back.

As the man drives away, shaking his head in disbelief, I decide it's time to start tallying how many offers of help we are getting a day. I won't be able to include the number of people who are stopping to just simply ask, 'Where you going?' as that is literally too many to count. Already we are up to day five of the expedition, but I can clearly recall the offers of a lift we have had so far. In the first four days we had a total of eight people stop. So far today it has been two. Every time somebody stops to help us I want to say 'yes', but we keep on walking.

After another arduous day of walking, we enter the town of Ban Kao and find a temple sitting on the outskirts. Entering the grounds of Wat Ban Kao, we seek out the monks.

We observe a lone monk sitting outside under a tree.

"Norn lup?" I say to the monk.

He nods, stands up and leads us to a building where the head monk, I'm assuming, is to be found. This monk speaks a little bit of English.

Luke says, "We are walking from Ban Pong to Sangkhla Buri and we would like to sleep at the temple if that is okay with you."

"You playing a game?" the monk asks suspiciously.

"No," I reply. What a strange question.

"You tourist?" the monk asks, scrunching his eyes to look at us closely.

"Yes," Luke replies, although we don't really class ourselves as tourists in the typical sense.

I am holding our map and the monk notices this. "You have map?" he asks.

"Yes!" Luke says, unfolding the map onto the floor. We explain to him our route, showing him where we have walked and where we plan to go. This seems to satisfy him.

"Okay," he says and takes us to the temple. I'm genuinely surprised that we are being allowed to sleep in the actual temple. The monk makes it very clear to me though that I am not allowed to step foot on the raised platform. Pointing to the platform he says, "Women, no. Buddhist."

"Okay," I reply.

Having left my shoes at the entrance of the temple (the common practice in all temples), I take my thongs out of my bag so that I can head over to the toilet block. The toilet block is simple; squat toilets and a big concrete tub of water that I'm once again incredibly thankful for. I head back to the temple and sit down to rest. The monk returns and as he enters the temple he notices I have shoes on my feet. In my tiredness I'd forgotten to remove my thongs.

"Shoe off please! Shoe off please!" he cries. I feel awful. I don't want to offend this monk who has opened up his temple to us. The monk then shows us a piece of paper. I have to giggle as it's filled with Thai sentences translated into English. I'm fairly certain he has popped onto Google Translate so that he can communicate with us.

Luke reads them out aloud, "Any problem call me." The monk beams proudly as we nod at his first sentence.

"Backpacks Buddhist Temple Sanctuary" Luke reads.

"What does that mean?" I say to Luke.

"I have no idea," he replies.

The monk is looking at us intently. I feel an urgent need to understand what this sentence means. Luke repeats the sentence to the monk. The monk nods. I'm really confused. Is he telling us there is a backpackers nearby where we could stay called *Backpackers Buddhist Temple Sanctuary?* We are nowhere near tourist land so that seems a little peculiar. Or is he asking us to remove our backpacks from the temple because it is a Buddhist sanctuary? I don't know! Neither does Luke. The monk is still keenly watching us. He grabs the piece of paper off Luke and reads the final sentence like a child reading out in front of the class, " Please ... have ... nice ... sleep ... in ... wat!" He wanders out of the temple seemingly satisfied that he has communicated to us well. Meanwhile we are completely baffled as to what the Backpacks Buddhist Temple Sanctuary could mean!

Luke announces he is going to have a wash. I take the time to check out my feet and the tender blisters that cover them. I hear the back door open and see that Luke is walking back in his undies, "Forgot my towel!" he exclaims, making his way to the other end of the temple to retrieve it. At that very moment I look out the open front doors to notice the monk returning with bottles of water.

"The monk is coming!" I whisper madly to Luke who makes a mad dash for the back door. There is nothing I can do to help this situation. I watch as Luke, clad only in Bonds undies, sprints the length of the wat. I can only hope that his long pasty white legs will get him out of sight before the monk enters through the front doors. It's a close call but thankfully Luke makes it in time. The monk thought that having shoes on inside was bad. Imagine if he had seen a half naked white man running around his temple!

Our sleep that night is broken by barking dogs. Loud and fierce, they don't sound friendly. I step outside to see what is going on and find myself faced with a pack of dogs foaming at the mouth, glaring at me through the darkness. I tread backwards slowly and decide to put up with the barking. It's a long night and we are both exhausted when we rise at 6am. The dogs are still prowling the temple grounds so we avoid them as we make our way to where the monks live. The monk from yesterday is waiting for us with a plastic bag. Inside are two cans of iced coffee and some plantain chips.

"You go Wang Pho?" the monk asks.

"Yes, we will be," I reply.

"My friend, Wang Pho Wat!" says the monk smiling from ear to ear.

Last night we didn't understand the monk's statement, 'Backpacks Buddhist Temple Sanctuary'. After experiencing the hospitality I think he was saying the temple is a sanctuary for backpackers. I'm falling in love with this country and its people. The generosity, kindness and friendship we have experienced so far are impressive. I feel I have a lot I can learn from these people. We farewell the monk, pick up some hefty sticks and exit the temple guarding ourselves from the territorial dogs with our make-do weapons.

About one kilometre down the road are early morning markets. The place is buzzing with farmers selling their fresh produce. Elderly ladies watch over their pots bubbling with rice, vegetables and eggs. Petite young women watch us closely as we glance into their fresh fruit baskets with limes, papayas and small sweet bananas. Locals are purchasing rice puddings wrapped in banana leaves as an early morning treat. I love local *talad nat*, as markets give an authentic experience of a place. The Ban Kao talad nat is for the locals and is about as authentic as you can get. Weaving through the stalls is enlivening my senses. The sights, smells, sounds are foreign and I love barely recognising anything that is for sale. We stop to buy some fried banana delights from an intriguing lady. Sitting cross legged on a wooden cart. She is grinning widely at us. Her entire face is painted white. She is wearing bright red lipstick and her teeth are as crooked as the Leaning Tower of Pisa. Further down the road we taste the donuts to find that in fact they are just little lumps of fried batter, greasy and sickly. My stomach immediately curdles when they hit it and I am forced to make an emergency toilet stop in the bush by the road – not pretty.

Today the sky is bright blue and I can tell it's going to

be a real scorcher of a day. With no shade on the road, we are going to find the ground will reflect the sun's blistering rays directly onto our faces. The sun is tormenting me and as the day progresses things are only getting worse. Luke is almost unable to walk due to his blisters. Today it is his turn to be at the rear while I'm up ahead. I have to remind myself to stop, turn and check where Luke is. He is going incredibly slowly. I wait for him to catch up. "This is killing me," Luke moans in obvious agony.

"I can see something up ahead, I'm not sure what it is but hopefully we can stop there to rest and have lunch," I tell Luke. His eyes tell me he doesn't want to go on, but I know it's best we continue because if we stop here we have no shade and nowhere to sit. So we keep on walking. I power on ahead secretly hoping that I've made the right decision. I know we are pushing Luke's feet beyond what we should if we want them to have any chance of recovery.

Finally, I can see what is ahead. A temple. Thank God! We can have a good rest here. I enter the grounds and find a place to sit. Luke reaches the temple about twenty minutes later. He is wrecked. As we rest, people in utes start arriving at the temple and setting up stalls. It seems it is market day. We are eternally grateful for this as it means we are able to buy coke in a bag (Thai take away style where they literally pour the coke directly into a small plastic bag) and ice-cream. It's the surprises like this that make you appreciate every single moment of discomfort leading up to unexpected sugary delights.

At 2.30pm we continue walking and the conditions are horrendous. Determined not to give up, we deny the offer of lifts we get from people. One man is insistent we get into his car. Our appearance must be shocking and he is obviously concerned for our well-being. I'm sweaty and grimy. Meanwhile, Luke looks like death. I can feel the air-conditioning escaping from the open car window and it is so hard not to get in. We convince him to let us be and he drives off probably thinking, 'They have no chance!'

We are unsure if there is a temple in the approaching town so we decide to try and camp by the river. The River Kwai is still with us and a chance to dip in it sounds pretty fantastic to me. The problem is we can't find an access to it. The closer we get to the town of Lum Sum, the less likely it is we will find a spot to camp. What are we going to do? A car stops. The people can't speak English but want to help us by giving us a lift. But we can't do it. Luke is not doing so well. His blisters are horrendous and the heat has really taken it out of him. I'm worried. He looks at me and his eyes are saying, "Get me the hell off this road Rachel." But no matter how hard it gets, we both know we will always refuse these offers. We keep walking, Luke trailing along slowly behind me. The road just keeps on going, a never ending path of torment. Looking ahead I notice the top of a temple with its red roof and gold trimmings. It's a welcome sight.

"Luke! It's a temple!" I yell, pointing my finger down the road. His eyes light up but that's the only recognition I get that he has heard me. He is struggling with every step. Every ounce of energy and concentration is being used on moving each foot forward one step at a time. However we have survived another day and once again a temple, with its promise of a wash, rest and tranquility, has come to our rescue.

7

Max the Monk

"Strangers are just family you have yet to come to know."
Mitch Albom

I leave Luke to rest his feet and I approach two monks I can see in the distance. They see me as I wave but then turn around and walk behind a building. I assume they are going to get the head monk so I wait and wait. Eventually I peek my head around the building and find the monks hanging out their robes. I find it peculiar that they aren't curious as to why there is a *farang* wandering around the temple grounds. Surely it's not common.

"Norn lup?" I ask. The monk points to another group of monks who are seated in the distance. As I walk towards them, a gang of dogs bears down on me barking and snarling. I'm terrified but thankfully the monks come to my rescue yelling at the dogs in Thai. The dogs retreat but keep their evil eyes on me. When all is calm again, I turn to the monks and ask, "Norn lup?" These monks are attentive and it doesn't take long for them to make sense of my poor Thai. One of the monks leads us to a wooden building with a covered platform, perfect for us to sleep on. The monk leaves us to settle in.

To get to the toilet block I have to brave walking past dogs that are drooling at the mouth, intently eyeing me off. Thankfully the monks yell at any dog who dares to step toward me. When I come back from having a wash, Luke is sitting chatting to a young monk. "He is loving the Thai phrase book!" Luke says. When the monk sees me, he jumps up and says, "Oookaaay!"

"Where are we going?" I ask Luke as we start following the monk who is smiling from ear to ear.

"I think he is taking us to have some food but I can't be sure. His English is very basic."

The monk has his head deep in the Thai phrase book as we walk through the temple grounds. He occasionally turns to us to point out a word or phrase for us to read.

"What's your name?" I ask. A quizzical look comes across his face. "Name?" I try.

"Ah … Oookaaay … Max!" he proudly responds.

Max leads us to a makeshift restaurant on the road. We are fed fried rice while the locals look on with pride and intrigue. Max reads the newspaper at another table as he is not allowed to eat after midday or with anyone who is not a monk. At the end of our meal, Max pays the bill. We are slightly confused at the situation but incredibly grateful for the proper dinner. Next is a tour of the temple grounds. We are exhausted but Max's excitement and enthusiasm to show us his home is a force to be reckoned with. Max is going to keep us busy.

With sign language and minimal English, we are able to communicate with Max but it's tiring. Each interaction takes time and requires a lot of patience. Max is drawing something in the sand which looks like a circle.

"Tum?" he says, "You see?" We have no idea what this means. The Thai phrase book is badly set out and practically useless. The Thai section is spelt with the English alphabet which means Max can't find the word he needs. Thanks *Rough Guides*.

I try to understand what word he is saying, "Tum?" I ask.

"Tum!" Max cries.

I can't quite understand.

"Tum?" I try again.

"Tum!" Max cries. This is getting frustrating for all of us. I take the phrase book from Max and look up the T words in the Thai section. I find a word spelt Tâm. I can't show the word to Max because it won't mean anything to him. So I try and say it, "Taam."

"Oookaay!!" Max nods and grins. It appears to be a cave he wants to show us! Max looks at us earnestly waiting for our answer. We are both really keen to see the cave. The problem is Luke's feet are in a bad way and he is wearing thongs, not great attire for a jungle walk. We didn't know we were embarking on a full blown adventure when we said 'yes' to dinner, but nothing is going to stop us from taking up this opportunity to spend time with Max the Monk!

"Okay!" we tell Max. He is overjoyed and briskly walks out of the temple grounds with us in tow. As we start walking down the road, thunder roars across the sky vibrating through our ears. Max turns to look at us. Pointing to the sky he says, "Rain come."

"How long will it take to walk to the cave?" I ask.

Another quizzical look. This is getting tiring. "Um, ten

minute? One hour?" I ask.

"Oookay!" Max nods, putting up two fingers.

"Two hours!" I gasp, what have we got ourselves into.

"Nooo," Max laughs, shaking his head.

"Twenty minutes?"

Max nods vigorously, "Oookay!"

We cross the railway line to find the dark, damp path which leads up to the cave. Max is going at such a swift pace, it is hard to keep up. Having walked a good seven hours today in the heat, with blisters, we are exhausted. The last thing we should be doing is traipsing through the jungle to a cave, especially in thongs, but when people open up their homes it's common courtesy to do things with them, even if you don't feel like it. If they want to feed you, you must eat even if you're full. If they want to show their photo collection, you must look at every photo with all the interest you can muster. If they want to take you on a walk that is two kilometres after having walked twenty kilometres already that day, you must walk it and hide any pain you are suffering as a consequence.

So, here I am; tired, in agony and in a cave. I have to admit though, the cave is impressive. A Buddhist shrine sits at its entrance and the remnants of previous monks are evident, everywhere. Candles, flowers, bottles, old matches are scattered around the shrine. The temperature difference between the cave and the outside provides a much needed release from the heat and humidity. Max takes us through his prayer ritual. We all light candles and place them at the altar. Max prays. I've visited caves before in Thailand and seen the remnants of monks' visits. It's a humbling moment to actually be here when it's occurring and I feel privileged. Although my beliefs are different to Max's, I feel he has a lot he can teach me, as does Buddhism itself.

When Max finishes his prayers, he turns and grins at us, "Oookaay." Max takes us for a walk around the cave. Thankfully he has brought a torch because it is pitch black in the cave, but with only one torch and our flimsy thongs, it's a challenge manoeuvring around. Max is patient and kind. I can tell by his smile alone that he is obviously loving every moment of this. Max points the torch light to show us a giant stalagmite, common in limestone caves, rising from the floor. Directly above it in the torch light, we can see the dripping minerals that form these structures. Its beauty that is normally hidden from human eyes, stands before me.

It's getting late and the storm is still looming so we decide to head back to the wat. Max is striding ahead once again and Luke's blisters are getting worse and worse. Rushing along behind Max, in thongs, on rough uneven ground is a bad idea, but not wanting Max to know how bad things are, Luke keeps a brave face and carries on. We manage to get back to the wat before the sky falls but our adventure is not over by any means.

Max takes us to his bedroom. What an experience – the inside of a monk's bedroom is not an experience many people have. Max's room is totally orange: the walls, the bed, the floor, everything! He has a mini shrine next to his bed and there are photos, cans of drink and packets of noodles placed around the walls. It is the quirkiest room I've ever seen. Framed and on the wall is a photo of a westerner and a letter including the envelope. Reading the letter I realise this is a traveller Max had met on the train. Max seems to be that type of person; one that would talk to a tourist on a train and ask them to write to him. Max is obviously very proud of this letter. When he notices us looking at it, he takes it down so we can have a closer look. The fact that he has even framed the envelope just shows how important this mail is to him. A letter from a *farang* is a treasure. I ask to take a photo with Max and he straightens up proudly; two tired, white siblings standing next to an overjoyed olive skinned monk dressed in his bright orange robe. The photo means a lot to all three of us. He writes down his address for us, beaming brightly at the prospect of another letter in the mail. Maybe we will also be framed and put on his wall. I wouldn't be surprised. An elderly monk comes to the bedroom door and says something to Max in Thai. Max replies, and as the monk leaves the room Max says, "Father."

"That's your father?" Luke confirms. Max nods.

"How long have you been a monk?" I ask. Max stares at me blankly tilting his head in confusion. "Wat ... how long ... um ... years ... here," I try.

"Oookaay ... five year!" Max beams.

"Wow!" Luke says.

Max ushers us to sit down. He has something else to show us. He pulls out an EVD player, not a DVD player, an EVD player. I have no idea what the difference is. He puts a CD in it and soon Eric Clapton's *Tears in Heaven* is drifting softly through the airwaves. Max sits with a huge grin on his face. I'm giggling uncontrollably because I can't believe I'm sitting in a monk's bedroom listening to *Tears in Heaven*. Max takes my giggles as an indication of approval and next plays Lionel Richie's *Endless Love*. This is the type of thing dreams are made of. You know the type – the dreams where your dad is Barry Manilow and you live in a giant crab. Well, I'm now living one of those dreams where I'm sitting with a monk in an orange room and listening to him sing his heart out to *Endless Love* by Lionel Richie.

We are completely exhausted and, much to Max's disappointment, tell him we will have to go to bed. We are terrified of walking back to our sleeping quarters in the dark because we have noticed the dogs are still prowling around. Max is proud to be able to walk us safely back to where we are to sleep and while we set up our beds he hovers around. By now we have learnt that Max is like an excitable puppy, and the more attention you give him, the less likely you are to free yourself from him. We need to put our mosquito nets up and have no string to do so. I know I'm going to have to ask Max so I look up the word for mosquito net in the Thai phrase book. "Móong?" I say *mosquito net* in Thai. Max nods.

"Chêuak?" I ask for string. Max nods.

"Have?" I ask in English. Max nods.

I sit and wait. Nothing's happening. Max is staring adoringly at us both. I try again but this time with actions, "Móong … Chêuak … have?"

This time he understands, "Oookay!" he exclaims. Jumping up, proud to have understood me and to be able to help, he scampers off like a puppy to find some string. Luke and Max put up our mosquito nets while I go to the toilet. When I return Luke is inside the net and Max is lingering on the outside. I crawl into the net to discover there are bugs galore on the inside of the net.

"What happened? The bugs are supposed to be

on the outside!" I ask Luke.

"The bugs got on the inside of the net when we were putting it up. I didn't want Max to realise because otherwise he would never leave. So I got inside and turned the lights off but he just won't go. He keeps finding excuses to stay. I kept saying goodnight but it didn't work. He passed me my torch, then ran and got a bottle of water and passed that through to me. He is obsessed with us!"

I have to laugh – a lot. Max the Monk is in love, with us. It is sweet. But when you have walked a seven to eight hour day in 40° heat, with blisters, and know you have to do it all again tomorrow, a cute little monk persisting with kindness starts to get a little irksome. Max lifts up the mosquito net, peers in at us with his puppy dog eyes and points to his watch.

"We are getting up at 5.30am," I tell him.

"Oookaay!" He smiles and waves goodnight. I have no doubt Max will be ready and raring to go outside our mosquito net at 5.25am tomorrow.

∞ ∞

I'm right. It is 5.25am and Max is bright eyed and bobbing on his feet outside our mosquito net. Max wants us to join him on his collection of alms. We would love to, but we decide not to. We need to get an early start. At 6.30am we depart the wat with Max by our side. It looks like Max is heading in the same direction as us. We have no idea how long Max will be with us and try to ask him, but he can't understand our question. So we keep walking and walking. Luke is not in a good way. His blisters are causing him immense pain. Trying to keep up with the brisk pace of Max is making it so much worse. Luke eventually crumples into a heap on the side of the road.

"I can't keep up Rachel. I'm feeling so ill." He drinks some water, puts some toothpaste in his mouth and stands back up. "Ok, lets keep going," he says, "but don't let Max know something is wrong."

About two kilometres down the road I have a sudden thought, "Luke did you remember your camera charger?" Luke has been making the most of electricity at the wats we've stayed at to recharge his camera batteries. It's been a real blessing for Luke not to have to worry about running out of battery. From the look on Luke's face I can tell I am now in for a long walk back to the temple.

"Oh, crap," Luke says. I try to explain to Max what has happened and therefore now what needs to happen, but it is a lost cause. So while Luke hangs back with Max and tries to explain, I start walking the two kilometres back to the temple. We are on a deserted road but in the distance a dot appears. It is a motorbike. I stick my thumb out and then in desperation wave my arms around leaping into the air. The motorbike pulls up alongside me. Sitting atop is an elderly man wearing a large brim hat made of straw, his eyes are warm and the lines on his face tell a story.

"Wat Lum Sum?" I say, pointing in the direction of the temple.

"Wat Lum Sum!" he nods.

"Wat Lum Sum?" I say again but this time I point to his motorbike and myself.

"Wat Lum Sum!" he nods again, smiling wide.

I climb onto the back of the motorbike and hug the man from behind. I feel safe with this Thai farmer. We arrive at the wat and I run inside to get the charger. The man waits for me and then takes me back to where Luke and Max are.

I don't think the man had any idea what I was doing, but we have the camera charger and I am grateful for the man's kindness.

We continue walking and arrive at Wang Pho bridge at around 7.15am. The railway disappears around the cliff and Luke and I know the infamous Death Curve lies around the bend. This is the moment we have been anticipating. I never thought we would be standing here with a monk named Max. But I'm glad we are.

"Wang Pho?" Max asks, pointing down the railway track.

"Yeah ..." I reply, slightly unsure of myself.

Max confidently walks ahead and turns to make sure we are following.

As we set off behind his bright orange robe, Luke says, "This is it, Rachel. The moment we have been waiting for!" Indeed it is! Of the six hundred and eighty trestle bridges built by the POWs, the one at Wang Pho was the most intimidating of them all.

The current bridge is the original constructed by hand, without any mechanical help. Anchored to the cliff wall the bridge is about two hundred metres long with a vertical cliff on the right, and a sheer drop to the jungle floor on the left. It's a striking, yet daunting, picture. In the distance I can see the calm River Kwai dotted with fbating villages creating a welcoming sense of tranquillity.

Luke and I are both anxious. The next two hundred metres or so will be us, an old bridge, and a sharp drop to the jungle floor. Despite our fears and anxieties of the unknown, walking along the Wang Pho Bridge proves not to be scary at all. There are planks of wood forming a path (possibly because this bridge is crossed often by locals, such as Max on his daily collection of alms) which means that walking is simple. No balancing on rotten sleepers or having to jump across large gaps. Also just the presence of Max means that I feel completely and utterly at peace with the bridge crossing. The bright orange monk robes have come to mean so much to me. Just the sight of Max's robe ahead gives me peace, hope, comfort and security. Once we have crossed the bridge we pass Krasae Cave and enter tourist city. There are little Thai ladies waiting for the daily horde of tourists to arrive so they can sell them overpriced t-shirts and souvenirs. We buy a bottle of water that is three times the price we have been paying in the small towns. I'm not a fan and I'll be happy to get out of here. But before we do that, it is time for us to part ways with Max.

"Train, 8 o'clock," Max says pointing to the railway. He is such a sweetheart. Concerned for our safety on the railway, he is making sure we know when the next train is passing by. Knowing we will be walking directly on the railway track today, I'm thankful for the information.

"Ok thanks," I say looking at my watch noting that it is in half an hour.

"Thank you so much for everything Max. We have had fun," Luke tells Max.

Max asks for the guide book. He looks up a word and points to it. 'Good luck' it says.

"Oohh kop kun ka!" I thank him.

Max grins, "Oookaay!"

We start walking towards the railway line and Max turns to continue on his morning walk. As we reach the railway line and start to walk along it, I hear my name called out in that typical Asian style when L replaces R.

"Lachel!"

I look and Max is standing at the turn of the road. "8 o'clock!" Max yells pointing to his wrist.

"Yes, train at 8 o'clock! Thanks Max!" I yell back.

I smile. This is how I will always remember Max, standing on a dirt road, his bright orange robe creating a stark contrast against the brown surroundings, tapping his wrist in an earnest manner.

Max nods, smiles and turns, walking into the distance. He is running very late. I imagine he will be eating by himself at the wat today as he is sure to arrive at the temple much later than all the other monks. I like to think he will eat with a smile on his face as he casts his mind back to the *farang* who entered his life so unexpectedly. Yesterday Max the Monk was a stranger, yet today he is part of our ever extending Thai family.

∞ ∞

I'm feeling lost without Max. The fear of walking along the railway anticipating trains bearing down on us has returned. I didn't realise how comfortable I had become having Max by our side. As frustrating as it was trying to communicate with him and trying to manage his enthusiasm, Max became a friend. I trusted him. I'm going to miss his poor English, huge smile and cries of 'Ooookaay ...'

We have only been walking about twenty minutes when Luke announces, "I don't think I can do this, my blisters are really really bad." We are standing outside a house that is under construction. No one is there so we go and sit on the stairs. Luke takes his shoes off to reveal his large, painful blisters. "I can't walk today Rachel," Luke says.

"So what do you want to do?" I ask him, concerned as to what this all might mean for our expedition. "I need to rest my feet. I can't walk one metre let alone another twenty kilometres. Maybe we should go back to Wang Pho and stay another night," Luke suggests looking miserable.

To be honest, I'm pretty devastated. I've had blisters on a walk before and I know that it can be the end of a trip. I'm not sure what to do.

"Let's bandage up your feet so that your foot has more support and the blisters aren't getting pressure or irritation with every footstep," I suggest. Luke agrees. I bandage his foot reminding myself that this is what expeditions are about and this is what being a sister is all about. Supporting one another and doing those things that don't appeal, like touching sweaty, smelly feet. As I'm doing this, a Thai workman arrives at the house. He smiles at us and starts his work. It's uncanny that he doesn't question why we are sitting on the stairs of this unfinished house.

Luke decides he will try walking. As we begin, he perks up significantly and I'm surprised when he says, "I don't want to speak too soon but if we walk slowly and take it easy, maybe we could make it to Nam Tok and then we could rest for two nights and have a full day off from walking." It's a big goal. Nam Tok is over twenty kilometres away, but the promise of a full day's rest if we do so is a big morale lifter.

Since leaving Wang Pho, we have been walking on the railway and our current surroundings are very remote. We are passing tiny rural houses and the occupants are very surprised to see us. I spot a house with a seat out the front so we take the opportunity to sit down. A girl from the house comes out to see what we want. Though they can't speak English, they understand us when we say Nam Tok and mimic walking on the spot. The girl rushes inside and brings out two cold glasses of water. At this stage I don't care anymore where the water has come from, I gulp it down grateful for every drop.

We keep walking. Over the morning the sun has climbed into a cloudless sky. It's a hot day and we are struggling in this heat. We come to a path and decide to leave the railway for a second. It doesn't take long until we are lost. We have walked onto a fairly large property with a fancy looking house. We stumble across an elderly lady doing gardening. She is startled by the sight of us but when we make a train sound she is pleased to be able to help. Jabbering away in Thai, she leads us further into the property and then points up a hill. We can see the railway track at the top of it. We return the favour of jabbering away in a foreign language telling her how grateful we are for her help.

The opportunity to meet locals in amongst their real lives deep in Thailand is just what I wanted from this trip. And, like the explorers before us, we are communicating with them despite the fact we don't speak the same language. I love it. We climb the hill and meet the railway. What we find is a long bridge disappearing around a mountain edge. I'm suddenly very nervous. We have no idea how long this bridge is. If a train comes while we are on it, there is nowhere to go. The bridge is metres off the ground and dense jungle is directly beneath it. If we have to jump off it, we are going to get seriously hurt. Medical attention is a long way from this remote location.

"Don't we have a train timetable?" Luke asks. We do! I have totally forgotten about the timetable I picked up back in Bangkok. According to the timetable, there is a train coming by in one hour.

"But the trains are never on time," I say to Luke.

"But they are never early are they?" says Luke. That is true; they are never early and nearly always late.

"So we at least have an hour," I comfort myself.

"I'll go first while you wait. Then you can yell to me if a train is coming," Luke suggests.

"Okay." I'm freaking out and the heat isn't helping. Sweat pours down my face as I watch Luke make his way across the bridge. I feel so vulnerable at these times. I really hate crossing the bridges.

"It's okay, you can come," Luke yells back to me.

On this section of the railway we are completely closed in by cliff on our right and jungle on our left. If a train does come things are going to get interesting. We eventually come across a small village where we leave the railway to walk on the road running parallel. I'm thankful to get off the railway because my blisters are starting to flare up. Luke seems to be doing okay but I do wonder how much of his struggle he is keeping inside. Now that we are back on the road, cars are stopping again to offer us lifts. When we tell them we are walking to Nam Tok, they are shocked. We have recently learnt the phrase for 'Is it far?' – glai mai – which means we can try and ask people how far away places are. Today when we ask, "Nam Tok ... glai mai?" the answer is always "Glai!!!!!" It's making me anxious.

How far are we going to be walking today? We have realised the map we are currently using is of no help. It was made in 1988. A lot has changed here since then. So our only real guidance is from road signs written in Thai and people who only speak the Thai language. It's proving challenging.

As the day drags on, we start to see the weather changing before our eyes. In the distance, grey rain clouds are moving across the land, creating large shadows. Surrounding the clouds is bright sunshine. I'm hoping we won't get caught in this rain cloud. Clouds opening up and dropping their bundle is fascinating to watch but would be awful to be caught in.

All day we have held on to the belief we are going to make it to Nam Tok. This has given us the motivation to keep walking. It's now afternoon. It's been a very long day. We pass a wat but after some discussion decide to continue to the town so we don't have to do any walking tomorrow. As long as Luke is keen to keep on walking, so am I. But I can tell that Luke is not doing well. The problem is neither am I. So I can't console him as I'm using everything within me just to move my feet forward. We reach a field and can see the highway and the town of Nam Tok on the other side. I tell myself that life begins at the end of your comfort zone. But I'm pretty sure Luke feels as though his life is ending. He went beyond his comfort zone at 8.30am this morning. I consider getting the camera from Luke to do some filming, but I'll be honest, that is the last thing I feel like doing. So I don't. I'm positive I'll regret that later. Luke's pace is excruciatingly slow. His face is showing signs of breakdown. We are both moving forward in a lackadaisical manner. We are both over it. It is possibly one of the longest walks of our lives so far. Though our destination is only about one kilometre in the distance, the pain and misery we are both experiencing is making it a living hell. Damn these blisters.

I don't know how, but after twenty kilometres and ten hours, we walk into the town of Nam Tok feeling very sorry for ourselves. I never want to walk another step. Luke is broken.

Thankfully we are going to stay in Nam Tok for two nights to allow ourselves to rest and recuperate. We need it.

8

A Reality Check

"In the cutting the scene became completely fantastic.
Men toiled and sweated and were driven mercilessly.
Men were flogged and men collapsed ...
Japanese and Koreans threw themselves into a frenzy
of efficiency and terrorism.
Men were battered. Limbs were broken. Men died."
Gunner Kenneth Harrison - 4th Anti Tank Regiment (Australian)

The POWs didn't know Nam Tok as Nam Tok. Back then it had a different name. Even the name Thailand is new. Prior to 1939 the country was Siam. This is what the POWs knew it as and most still refer to it as Siam today. Nam Tok was called Tarsao and it had a large POW hospital, a true living hell. It had the reputation of being a place where men were sent to die. If you had been at Tarsao during the war you would have seen collections of attap huts. Inside these huts would have been bodies of men wasting away stricken with malaria, dysentery, cholera, beri-beri and tropical ulcers. The smell of death and disease would have overpowered you.

Today the town of Nam Tok is complete with shops, streets and houses. Luke and I found a cheap, but not so cheerful, hotel to stay in and have slept, eaten and rested for two days. The POWs didn't get much sleep, food or rest but rather suffered daily until their impending death arrived. Our blisters though painful and sore seem pitiful compared to the ailments POWs lived with in this town all those years ago. I don't spend too much time comparing because I realise that my experience is different. Watching my body deteriorate over the past five days of walking has opened my eyes to why the POWs suffered so terribly. Heat rash, blisters and sunburn are on our top list of daily problems. However, we are lucky. We can eat healthily and stop when we need to stop. The POWs' diet was so poor that their bodies were unable to recover from the simplest of illnesses. This resulted in sores becoming infected and the skin rotting away, even from a simple scratch. Being in Nam Tok has allowed me the time and space to appreciate, in the light of our own experiences, the history of men who tolerated the intolerable.

Nowadays, Nam Tok is the end of the railway. The POWs completed building the Thai-Burma line but soon after the war the track was bombed and pulled apart. Today the only operating section is from Ban Pong to Nam Tok. It is time to get back out there and start walking but before we move on from Nam Tok we want to visit the very end of the railway line. I am surprised by my feelings about leaving the railway behind. The line has become a symbol for me. It's given me hope, security and something I could rely on. How different this must be from the POWs' outlook on it. I can only imagine that the POWs saw the railway as a symbol of torture, death and captivity; a daily reminder that they were not going home and that this was their life now.

Nam Tok station is simple and quiet. A few stalls selling

food stand outside and locals are sitting waiting for the morning train to leave. The line itself continues past the platform for about fifty metres and then it ends. No more railway track, just jungle. For us too, there will be no more railway track. What is ahead is unknown.

As we pass through the last section of Nam Tok we come across roadside stalls of fruit and vegetables tempting travellers like ourselves to stop and buy. With mangoes at an incredible 10B each (30 cents) I can't say no. Fully charged by the promise of mango for lunch, we start walking along Highway 323 which runs from Kanchanaburi all the way to Three Pagoda Pass at the Thai-Burma border. People from all over the country use this highway daily. What it gains in offering convenience, it lacks in character. Gone are the tiny villages occupied by simple, friendly Thai families. Gone are the smiles and waves of hardworking rural folk tending their crops.

Walking along the highway I quickly learn one important rule – try to stay alive! Many things could be said about Thais and their driving but my main observation is, they're *dangerous*. Thai drivers ignore all traffic signals, traffic lights, the yellow and white lines in the middle of the road, the road itself. Thai drivers are incredibly impatient and will overtake anyone in front of them. They will flash their lights and honk their horns which tells the cars in front 'I'm coming through no matter what or who you are.' This overtaking will occur on blind corners, brows of hills, anywhere. It makes no difference if there are double unbroken lines in the middle of the road or if another vehicle is approaching in its own fast and unpredictable manner. They will also overtake by going onto the shoulder and it doesn't matter if there are two *farang* walking there. Walking along Highway 323 is terrifyingly insane.

To make matters worse, about half an hour into our walking we experience our first rain of the expedition. We are walking up into the mountains for the first time and the change in weather is dramatic. It is no longer a stifling 40°c. Instead it is wet and humid. Because it is not as hot, we are able to walk at a decent pace and cover good ground.

Not wanting to push ourselves too hard, when we come across a wat that is three kilometres from Hell Fire Pass we decide to ask if we can stay there. It's been a wet day and a scary day. The first monk we find on the temple grounds has a bizarre response to our favourite question of, "Norn lup?"

"No, women no. Men ok," is the monk's answer.

The monk goes and fnds another monk to help communicate with us. Back home I had actually printed off some phrases that I thought might come in handy. So far none of them have, but I decide to bring them out again to give it another go. I point to the phrase in Thai that says, 'Can we put up our tent in your property?' I want them to know that we are not asking to stay *in* the temple. It's just reassuring to know people will be around if we need them. The monks talk amongst themselves and keep pointing south. I'm worried they are trying to direct us to a resort. But eventually the monk says, "Toilet okay, building no, tent okay." We are shown to a shelter which has a simple tin roof. It's perfect.

As we start to put up our tent, Luke has a revelation, "I

just realised that because my tent can be put up without pegs essentially it is a mosquito net. We don't need to string up our mosquito nets anymore we can just use the tent!" We feel kind of stupid when we realise just how simple an idea this is, but I'm just grateful we no longer need to use our fiddly mosquito nets. As we are putting up our tent the monk comes over to us and asks, "Kao?"

I'm starving so I reply enthusiastically, "Yes!" I had noticed a group of locals partying on the temple grounds and this is where we are directed to.

The group of people are infectiously friendly, incredibly generous and bubbling over with excitement. Luke and I sit down while ten pairs of eyes watch our every move. An old man with few teeth and kind eyes piles two plates with rice and gives us a bowl of Tom Yam soup each. It is scrumptious. The scent of lemon grass is infused in every mouthful. The taste of coconut is seducing my taste buds and the chicken is plump and juicy. I notice an old lady with a sweet smile and slightly erratic eyes chatting away to me in Thai. It is obvious that the others are telling her to leave me alone. I giggle into my soup. What an eccentric group we have stumbled upon. I look in the phrase book for a word I can use and find the phrase 'nice food'. "Aroy!" I chime. The entire group clap their hands, bend their heads back and cackle with glee. I think I've just made their day. The old man puts his two fingers together as if to say, "Are you two together?" In the phrase book I find the word for younger brother, "Norng Chai" I tell them. More cackling and throwing of body parts. These people are easy to please! They keep feeding us until we are well and truly full.

I wish I could speak Thai fluently. I want to tell them

just how grateful I am for the free meal. Instead of eating packet noodles, we have been given a feast of homemade Thai gourmet food, but all I can say is "Kop kun ka" thanking them over and over again. We return to our tent and realise that because we stopped walking at 3pm today we have plenty of free time. I'm thankful. We are left alone for the rest of the day and the peace and quiet are not something I take for granted.

I've woken at 5am to the sound of rain pelting down on the tin roof above me. I'm now envisaging a day of wetness as I slowly rise to pack down the tent. Thankfully we are under the shelter otherwise our tent would be wet through. It's the little things like not having to pack away a wet tent that make me thankful we can stay at temples. By the time we have packed and are ready to go, the rain has eased off. The group of locals from yesterday are back again and have been setting up since 5.30am. As we start to leave they notice us and yell, "Kao!" More food? Yes please! Delicious food, inquisitive eyes and cackling laughter is a great way to start the day.

Full bellied and in high spirits, Luke and I walk the three kilometres to Hell Fire Pass and arrive just as it is opening. Thankfully we have moved onto one of our more useful maps and can see that the route we were planning to take actually goes through the museum grounds. We want to continue walking without coming back to the museum building. We realise this won't work when they hand us headsets and ask for a 500B deposit. While we are standing in reception sorting out where to leave our backpacks for the duration of our visit, a man with a thick Australian accent enters the building and hollers, "G'day girls!" to the ladies at the front desk.

As we are taking our shoes off to enter the museum, the man sees us and says, "Hi guys, how you going?" Looking at Luke's camera equipment he says, "You got some serious looking kit there! Are you some budding journalists or something?" Luke and I look at each other. Lately, we haven't been divulging our whole story to people we meet. From experience we have learned it takes too long to explain, and people tend to crinkle their faces in confusion.

However, this guy works here and might be able to help us so I say to Luke, "Off you go!"

As Luke starts to tell him what we are doing, the guy interrupts saying, "Oh, you're following the railway. Yes, I've seen you! I passed you in my car and I thought to myself those two are following the railway."

I'm slightly perturbed that people are now recognising us from the highway. Doesn't say much for our safety.

"I have a meeting to go to now but I'd be happy to chat to you in half an hour or so. My name is Simon by the way." With the promise of a further chat, Luke and I leave Simon and head down the path towards the infamous Konyu Cutting.

Hell Fire Pass is an important site for Australians. It was predominantly Australian POWs who were placed at this camp enduring 12 – 18 hour shifts without rest. The POWs had to make a forty metre cutting through the hard rock of the mountain. With no machines and dangerous dynamite to blast the rock, it was high-risk work. The Japanese called the place Konyu Cutting but the POWs had a different name for it. At night the light of the bamboo torches and bonfires created an eerie flickering light which cast shadows of the gaunt men onto the rock face. This led to the infamous nickname Hell Fire Pass. Today the site is so clean and tidy, it's hard to imagine what really happened here. As I walk through the forty metre cutting, I run my fingers along the rock wall. It's cool to touch and I feel a strange connection with the men who toiled day and night to create this gap in the mountain. Standing still, I crane my neck to the sky, and through the canopy I can see the sky peeking through. The sun's rays are creating a glow inside the cutting and I can see dust particles floating through the air. Listening to the headsets, I am overwhelmed by the stories being told to me by ex-POWs who were stationed at Hell Fire Pass. One very famous POW was located here, Sir Ernest Edward 'Weary' Dunlop. Described as a man who was so well mannered you had no idea what he was thinking, Weary was an Australian surgeon who exhibited strong leadership skills. In POW camps, Weary was able to restore morale and saved many lives. As Luke and I take a seat at the Kwae Noi Valley Lookout, I listen to words from Weary Dunlop's journal coming from the headset.

"The evening and the morning positively hurt with their beauty. Especially the lovely quarter hour before dawn when the whole sky is aglow with brilliant crimson bands showing through the clearly etched foliage. A brilliant atmosphere and the softest of pale blue."

The view at Kwae Noi Valley Lookout is just that. It

positively hurts. The indigo mountains are lined up on the horizon with the iridescent jungle below. The POWs had an amazing backdrop to work against and it's encouraging to hear Weary's words of beauty and hope. Within minutes of our sitting looking out at this gorgeous view, the weather changes. One minute we can see all the way to the horizon. Next, purple-black clouds have rolled in and the rain is sluicing its way across the valley. Thankfully we are sitting under a shelter because those clouds are heading our way and when the rain arrives it is heavy and hard. Not able to go anywhere without getting completely saturated, we remain under the shelter and watch the rain do its thing. Rivulets of rain water spill down the leaves of trees onto the jungle floor, racing towards the river we can see in the distance. The rain doesn't last long. The clouds move on, the view returns and the humidity doubles as the rainwater evaporates into the sky; the hydrologic cycle in action.

Surrounded by monsoonal rains like this has to be experienced to be believed. The rain falls insidiously to begin with and evolves into an overpowering effect where one's mind and body is stupefied. The heat created by the evaporation of rainwater is overpowering and regaining composure takes time.

Having escaped these effects by staying dry under the shelter, we venture back into the wild and walk back up to the museum building. When we reach the stairs that climb to the museum, I notice that there is another path heading in a different direction. I wonder where that goes. Maybe that is the path we need? Back at the museum we take a look at our map and realise that the path we had been planning to follow, the one that goes directly through the museum grounds, is actually closed for repair according to the museum signs.

"Did you notice that path at the bottom of the stairs?" I ask Luke.

"Yeah I did, do you reckon that will take us to the river?" That is all we need really, to get to the river, so we can follow it. In fact, when we were at the lookout we could see a temple on the other side of the river.

"Simon is our best bet I reckon. He will be able to give us some direction for sure," I say to Luke.

Knocking on Simon's door we find that he is more than keen to invite us in and talk to us. Handing us information on Hell Fire Pass, he tells Luke, "You'll need that for your documentary!"

"Oh, thanks, " says Luke, "we were wondering if you could help us with where to go next. We need to get down to the river and we are wondering if this path on the map still exists and will it take us to the river?"

Simon takes one look at our map jumps up and declares, "What you want is a proper map!" A proper map? I'm not sure what is wrong with ours. It's 1:50,000 scale which means it's pretty detailed and it's recent. I think our map is pretty good. But if he has a better one I'm keen to see it. Simon takes us to his quaint little house which is underneath the museum building. Western in all aspects, it is a very comfortable looking home. In his office he has a collection of WWII photos and artefacts on the walls. One of them is a map which he pulls off the wall for us to look at. It is a very old map once owned by a POW. Though it is very interesting to see a map that had belonged to a POW, I can't imagine how such an old map will be of use to us. Names of places have since changed, new roads built and old roads destroyed. Simon seems to be oblivious to the original question we asked him about a path that will take us down to the river, but not only that, Simon doesn't seem to know what he is talking about!

I try to ask him again, "So is there a road that we can follow down to the river?" Simon's response is a long string of instructions that are not an answer to my question and don't make much sense.

Pointing to a section of the map called *Chong Khao Khat* he informs us, "This is where we are now. You see you need to be able to read the Thai!" The thing is my Thai is good enough to know that *Khao* means mountain and we are definitely *not* on a mountain. In fact the mountain he is mentioning is about 1-2km north. Just like it says on both of the maps!

"How long have you worked at Hell Fire Pass?" I ask.

"Nine years," he replies. We listen politely to more of his misinformed guidance, including telling us we need to head back to the highway, until we can finally remove ourselves from his home and company. We thank him for his help and say goodbye.

Luke looks at me when we are out of Simon's sight, "You know he was wrong, right?!"

"Yes," I reply.

"Oh good. That mountain he was talking about is not where he says it is."

We decide we will head back down the wooden stairs and try the path I noticed earlier. Slight issue: the path will take us straight past Simon's office with his wide window looking out onto the Hell Fire Pass paths below. We don't want him to see us as he will realise we are going against his advice. In a stealthy manner, Luke and I sneak past his window, trying to stay low and not attract attention. At the junction, we take the path to the left while all other tourists take the path to the right towards the Konyu Cutting. This path takes us out to a main road which looks as though it will take us down the mountain. It is exactly what we need. It's a mystery why Simon did not mention this path to us.

Walking down this road is agony. The steepness of the road is taking its toll on my knees and pulling the muscles in my calves. I find that walking diagonally helps, from one side to the other. The stress on my body is relieved by this alternate way of walking down a mountain. It's a long way down and the further we go, the more my nerves are kicking in. In all honesty, we have no idea where we are going. Further down the road, we can see a gang of dogs. Although they are accompanied by an owner, we don't trust them for a minute. We both arm ourselves with sticks we find on the ground and brace ourselves for a fight. The dogs see us approaching and seem to have a consensus among themselves which, for some unknown reason, is to let us pass. I don't know why this is but I'm grateful as the owner didn't lift his eyes once, so I don't think we could have relied on him for rescue.

We pass the Hintok River Camp which is obviously a resort that sits on the river. It's interesting how disinterested I am in staying at a place like that. After the temples we have stayed in, I'm almost ruined for staying in a hotel, motel, resort, even a backpackers ever again. Staying in the houses of locals has been a fantastic experience, one that not many people have, and I can only hope that we won't have to resort to a … well … resort!

It's really hot, as usual, and Luke is busting for the toilet.

"I reckon just go ask one of these locals if you can use their toilet," I say, as we pass a line of houses.

In the front yard of one house is a wooden bench with a shade. I sit down while Luke contemplates his bladder issue. The next door neighbour has obviously seen us sitting in his neighbour's yard and comes to see if we are okay. Luke takes the opportunity to ask if he can use his toilet.

When Luke returns he says, "The guy has asked us if we would like a coffee."

Keen for some more local interaction, we take up the man's kind offer. His house is very simple and made of concrete. Over coffee, we discover he has been building it himself for a while but has run out of money. However, with four walls, a ceiling, a simple kitchen and bathroom and one large room, I figure what more do you need. The man's name is Wireke and I like him already. "Your lunch finish?" Wireke asks.

"No we haven't had lunch yet," I say, craving food that isn't noodles. Noodles are all we have been eating when we haven't been getting fed by the monks or friendly locals.

"Okay, I have noodle!"

We enjoy a quiet lunch with Wireke. He keeps saying, "Anytime you here, you welcome to stay." I so wish we could take him up on his offer, but we also feel the pressure to keep walking. Some days it's hard to choose between keeping to our walking deadline or spending time with the people we meet.

I'm sad to leave and as we walk up the narrow path behind his house I hope we have made the right decision. It is a tough climb. The mountainside is incredibly steep and it's really hot. We reach the path we were looking for and turn left. This path should take us along the river to a village about three or four kilometres away. It's not a clear path, and dense jungle is making it difficult to walk. My feet keep getting caught in vines that are crawling along the path and I'm getting seriously annoyed, yelling out in frustration.

The path is becoming more and more overgrown the further we go along it.

"Look at that!" Luke says.

I look down to see a rotting piece of wood. Further ahead I see more and realise they are all lined up in a similar manner. It dawns on me – we are amongst a section of the original railway. These rotting pieces of wood are actually wooden sleepers hidden amongst the green and browns of the jungle floor. It is a surreal moment. Not set up for tourists in any way, we are seeing the railway as it is, rotting, lost, forgotten. We follow the track for a good kilometre and, as we do, the jungle is getting thicker and thicker.

Luke stops suddenly, "Where is the path?" I've been intently watching my feet trying not to trip over anymore roots or vines. I hadn't even noticed there is no longer a path; it's just jungle.

"I'll go ahead and see if I can find it," Luke offers.

As he ventures into the jungly scene before us, I take in our surroundings. We are completely consumed by foliage. Ahead there are massive boulders that need to be climbed and trees towering towards the sky. There is no way we are going to be able to find our way. It's also 4.30pm and I am not interested in getting lost in the Thai jungle.

Luke is still climbing his way through the wilderness and I'm suddenly overcome with fear. "Luke I don't think you should go any further!" I yell.

"Nah it's okay, I'm just going to check out what's over this edge."

"Please don't! What if you fall? This is how people die!"

"I reckon we can make it though!" Luke yells back as he inches closer to the edge of a large boulder.

"Pleeeaaasssse come back." For a moment, I flash back to our childhood …

Luke is on his **BMX** at the top of a very steep road. The road has many side streets coming off it and a car could come at any moment. Luke careers down at full speed pedalling furiously to gain more momentum. I'm standing at the bottom, a hundred metres away, praying. He whips past me and the gush of wind almost knocks me off my feet. He has lived to survive another day. Now I've seen it's possible so I decide to give it a go too …

Snapping back to reality, I realise that though I've always been a risk-taker, Luke has always overstepped the boundaries in terms of physical risk more than me. I'm also now almost thirty years old and I have a husband to go home to. I'm hoping Luke will realise that venturing into this jungle is not a good idea.

When Luke turns back I'm more than relieved. With more of an insight, Luke has now realised the terrain is steep, tangled with vines and disorientating. Not only that, there is something about this place with its perilous surroundings that is not comforting. I didn't come here to get lost, to die far from home in a scary jungle, or to seriously injure myself because of a stupid decision. We have no choice but to turn back.

9

Good Lucky

"Never shall I forget the days I spent with you.
Continue to be my friend, as you will always find me yours."
Ludwig van Beethoven

"What are we going to do?" I ask.

"Should we go back to Wireke and stay the night?"

"He would love it wouldn't he!" We both grin at the thought of rocking up on Wireke's doorstep again. He would be so excited. In fact, I can't think of anything I'd rather do at this moment or anywhere else I'd rather be.

We arrive back on Wireke's doorstep slightly embarrassed at having turned back but in good spirits once we see Wireke's face again. He is confused to see us. "We got lost!" Wireke smiles kindly. His t-shirt hangs off his small frame; his glasses perch upon his flat Asian nose; and he waddles inside with his bowed legs. As I follow him, I notice he also has quite a severe limp. His body may be old and frail, yet my young heart is growing fond of this quirky and interesting man.

"Where you sleep tonight?"

"If it's ok with you we would like to sleep here?" Luke asks.

"You sleep in resort, okay. You sleep here, okay."

"Here is nice," I reply.

"When I give you noodle I feel happy. You can stay here. You are welcome."

Wireke is obviously really excited to have us in his home. We take a seat on the floor and he starts to talk of his past. I'd been intrigued by this man but now I'm captivated by his story. It seems we are staying at the house of a man who was part of the team that cleared the jungle from the Thai-Burma railway so that the Hell Fire Pass Museum could be opened. I'm at a loss for words. We have stumbled across a Thai local who is a part of the Death Railway story. Considering our entire motivation for this walk is the Death Railway, I'm feeling flummoxed. For a journey that is being planned moment by moment, we couldn't have pre-planned it any better. The spontaneity of meeting Wireke makes it even more significant.

Wireke is hard to understand. Although his English is okay, he has a strong accent that makes it difficult to decipher, but I do manage to learn from him that he found bamboo legs, and other belongings of the POWs, left to rot in the jungle. All these artefacts now sit in the Hell Fire Museum. "I work with Rod Beattie to clear the railway," Wireke casually mentions.

"Really? We know Rod!"

"Well if you tell him my name, he know me!"

Wireke has only good things to say about Rod but as far as the manager of the Hell Fire Pass Museum goes, he is bitter. "The old manager, nice man. He have my name on signs to say I fnd these bamboo legs and other thing. But this new manager he not like me and he take my name away." Wireke is visibly upset about this and he talks at length about it.

When we tell him what we are doing in Thailand, he is amazed. "You walk this far?!" Shaking his head he continues, "Hintok Camp was on my land. Many prisoner of war here during those year. My parents lived in Thong Pha Phum during the war. I'm not sure if they see the Japanese. My parents die when I'm six year old."

It is a privilege to speak to someone who has connections, in some way, with the POWs. Many of the Thai's who had been around during the war would now be very old and not speak English. We have been fortunate to stumble across Wireke. "If Thai, Australian, Japanese, Korean … it don't matter. I like them all," he says.

I am inspired by his attitude. If only all people could be so forgiving. Wireke's story has a sad ending. "When I work on the railway, rock fall down onto my leg. I can't walk for 3 year." That explains the limp. Wireke hasn't worked a day since the accident on the railway clearing. He has to rely on his wife's earnings.

Wireke's wife returns home from work. She works at the Hell Fire Pass Museum and even saw us there this morning. I'm sure she is very surprised to see us in her home but you wouldn't know it. Wireke talks to her and she is pleased to have us stay. She brings out some mango for us to eat. Luke and I devour the mango in minutes. "You like the mango?" Wireke asks as we wipe the juice from our chins.

"Yes!"

"These mango I grow from tree out there," he points to his front yard.

"Mangoes are so expensive in Australia!"

"How much are they?"

"About $5, so 200B!"

"Oh, you know how much here? About 5B!"

Another reason to move to Thailand permanently. Mangoes are falling off trees in their thousands! I could eat mango for breakfast, lunch and dinner.

It is people like Wireke that are making this walk worth every step. Wireke's wife is already preparing dinner for us and in no time there is a feast laid out on a table. Rice, cabbage, chicken, corn and, of course, more mango. Wireke and his wife are not rich people; on the contrary, yet they have opened their home to us and fed us more than we could have ever imagined.

"More rice?" Wireke asks. He can't understand why we aren't eating all the rice dished up to us. The Thai's eat more rice than I thought a human could stomach. Our eyes are drooping with tiredness so we thank them for the meal and excuse ourselves to go to bed.

The large room within the house is separated by a curtain which gives Wireke and his wife their much deserved privacy. Luke and I set about putting up our tent. Wireke is very impressed with our make do mosquito net. It's moments like these that I feel like a rich westerner in an alien land. Wireke's house is so simple and he doesn't own much at all. Our tent seems so extravagant and colourful. It is the elephant in the room; a reminder that we come from different worlds. The tent, in my mind, is definitely needed though. All night the windows have been opened allowing all creatures great and small to enter the house at their will. Now that it is 'bed time', Wireke's wife closes the windows successfully trapping any bugs inside with us. As I lay out my sleeping bag, I hear something large crash into the tent. Fearing it to be a monkey, or even worse, an elephant, I turn slowly to see a humongous beetle about the size of my hand regaining consciousness on the outside of the tent. How thankful I am for the thin layer of material making a barrier between us. Meanwhile Wireke and his wife sleep on the floor with no protection. I'm sure they must be eating their fair share of bugs each night, involuntarily.

In the morning, whilst eating more noodles and mango, we show Wireke our map and ask if there is a road nearby that will take us to Sai Yok National Park.

"Yes, we have a road through the village and it go onto Sai Yok. Okay!" Wireke proudly tells us. He gives us his mobile phone number saying, "You have any problem you call me. Any problem."

It is time to leave and I am sad. Wireke and his wife have been so hospitable and friendly. They have made our stay comfortable. Not only are we leaving with full bellies and a bag filled with mangoes, but also a heart overflowing with affection for a man we only met the day before. We didn't spend a lot of time with Wireke but the short stay with him will go with me for the rest of my days. Before we leave, Luke interviews Wireke and films it, a great addition to the documentary Luke is planning to make. Our journey, inspired by the POWs who built the Death Railway, will now be complemented by our meeting Wireke and his own unique relationship with the railway.

"Good lucky with your trip!" Wireke says as he waves us goodbye from his front door. Good lucky – I think that encapsulates it all and I can't help but grin. My joy breaks through the morning mist as we walk down the road. I look back at Wireke standing watching us walk away and a lump appears in my throat. I'm humbled by people we are meeting on this journey. I am starting to realise that this walk isn't just about men who had died and survived an horrendous history. It is also about people, relationship, community. I am learning more than I had expected in ways I'd never imagined. I wipe the tears from my cheeks and focus on the farm we are approaching.

A family is staring at us. Already clueless about where to go, we pull out our map and Thai phrase book. The farmer walks with us to his field and points through it. Next thing we are trudging through the rice field getting muddier with each step. On the other side of the field we come to a path that goes directly up the mountain.

"That looks a lot like where we were yesterday," I say to Luke.

"Yeah, I'm not walking all the way up there just to turn back again."

It is immediately obvious we are not going to make it via the jungle. It is suicide. After a short conversation, we decide to return to the village and see if we can get a boat up river. On our map we can see the village Wang Nam Won which is further up the river and it joins onto the road we need. Walking back across the field we approach a house where some women are sitting out the front weaving baskets. Using our Thai phrase book we show one woman the word for 'boat' in Thai – reu-a. She understands 'boat' but as usual the phrase book fails us as she can't use it to help her communicate with us. What is the use of a phrase book having the Thai language organised in English alphabetical order? I'll tell you – there is no use! The lady manages to find the phrase "At the bottom of the road" which just happens to be on the same page as boat. Not fully understanding what she is trying to tell us, we eventually follow her like she asks us to. With about six kids in tow, we walk with her through the village to a house where she starts talking with a man. Whilst they are talking, a boy on a motorbike is instructed by them to go … somewhere. We are curious as to what is happening. A few minutes later the boy returns on the motorbike – with Wireke on the back! I feel really silly. The last thing Wireke had said to us was "Any problem call me!" and we hadn't.

He is noticeably upset. "I tell you to call me!" At least Wireke can now translate for us.

"So you want to have boat take you on river?" Wireke asks.

"Yes we want to go to Ban Wang Nam Won," Luke says showing them all the map. They take a good look at the map. The man is fascinated by it and asks where we got it. Wireke explains that we are at the house of the headman of the village. Apparently the headman does have a boat but is busy and about to go to a meeting down river. Desperate to get use of his boat, we press for Wireke to ask the man again. The headman eventually agrees to take us up river to Ban Wang Nam Won before he goes to his meeting. Not wanting to make the headman late, we rush down to the river, bid Wireke another farewell and clamber into the boat. As the boat putters away Wireke yells, "Call me if any problem! And please give man money for fuel, very expensive."

The river is tranquil, a nice rest from the stress of the morning. Looking at the terrain along the river, we know it would have taken us days to tramp through that jungle. In fact, I doubt we would have made it. Our decision to get a boat is another of our best. When we arrive at the village Wang Nam Won, the headman walks with us up the path. When he is satisfied we know where we need to go, he waves goodbye. I try to give him money for the fuel he has used but he won't accept it yabbering away in Thai and gesturing wildly as he steps back down the path. I am astonished. Rural Thai people are so different from the locals in the tourist traps of Thailand such as Bangkok, Phuket, Pataya and the islands. Most locals in those areas are out to scam you or overcharge. This headman has done us a huge favour and I am overwhelmed, once again, at just how generous and kind the Thai people are.

Walking along the Death Railway

Saying goodbye to Mai and her husband

Crossing the bridge over the River Kwai

A monk from Wat Na Kan on his collection of alms

Max the Monk

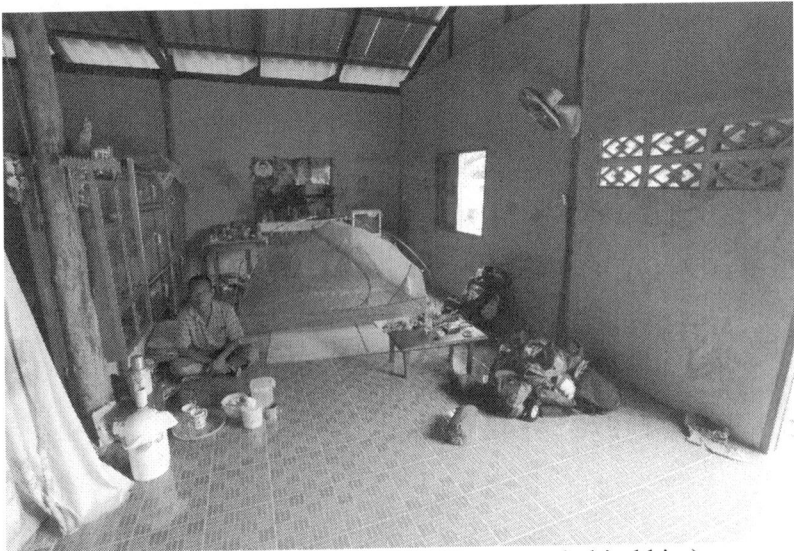

Wireke sitting in his little house (our tent set up behind him)

Celebrating Luke's birthday – in the middle of nowhere

A temple in a cave – Wat Tâm Sukow

10

A Lesson From
Mr. Banana Man

*"The real voyage of discovery consists
not in seeking new landscapes
but in having new eyes."*
Marcel Proust

In my mind I am still chugging down the river on a boat feeling as still and calm as the water that surrounds me. The birds are racing beside us trying to keep up; wind is carrying the cries of monkeys in the distance; splashes of water are creating droplets on my trousers. Reality though, is very different. The boat is, in fact, long gone. Instead we are deep in the jungle and only sporadic houses along the dirt road give us the confidence that we are not completely alone. And it's raining. For the second time on this walk we have had to put our rain ponchos on. Luke's is ripped already – piece of junk. At least it is only the second day of rain we have had so far. It could have been so much worse.

The dirt road we are following is going for miles. Every now and then locals pass us carrying long bamboo branches on makeshift wheelbarrows. They stare, whisper to each other and smile when we say, "Sawadee ka." Interacting with the Thai people in these remote areas is special. I'm certain they don't see many white people around here.

We stop for lunch at a deserted house. The family must be out working on their farm. We make the most of their shelter to protect us from the rain. There are a few dogs loitering under the shelter as well. One dog decides to sit at my feet. This isn't the type of dog you pat. There are ten million dogs in Thailand and many of them are ridden with rabies. Knowing my luck this is one of them. He seems harmless. By that I mean I don't feel threatened by an attack, so I don't try to get rid of him but I'll be avoiding any direct contact with him.

The POWs actually ate dog during their time in Thailand. Desperate times called for desperate measures. I guess when all you have been given by the Japanese is rotten, maggot infested meat, a dead dog doesn't sound too bad. But we aren't about to live out that part of the POWs story. Once again we have been blessed with food from locals. We tuck into the flesh of the juicy, plump mangoes Wireke gave us this morning. Our fingers are covered in the juice and it's dribbling down our chins. We look like two toddlers who smooshed their lunch all over themselves.

Luke and I wash our sticky hands in the rain puddles and then immediately realise this was a really dumb thing to do. "Washing in dirty water is how the POWs caught things like cholera and here we are washing our hands in puddles that these feral dogs could very well have just peed in," Luke remarks.

How stupid of us. I realise we are becoming a little too complacent. We have to remember that there are things here that could cause us harm. I rub some alcohol gel on my hands and silently say a prayer of protection. No more puddle handwashes for me.

Taking a look at the map, we can see we will soon come to a T junction at a village. According to the map, there is a path that cuts across the jungle from the village of Ban Maenam Noi to Sai Yok National Park. It'll be nice to be back amongst nature and not walking along a road for a while. Even though it is only a dirt road, I still long to walk through nature in its raw form.

Satisfied with our lunch of mango, and nervous that our fingers are possibly riddled with cholera, we decide it's time to get a move on.

When we reach the fork in the road, we can't see any obvious path heading into the jungle. Two car drivers see us at the intersection and stop to help. Their English is limited and they don't seem to understand that we want to find the jungle path. Instead they keep pointing down the road, "Sai Yok? This way." After we thank them for their help, they still linger around staring at us and our map. It can be hard to detach ourselves from helpful locals sometimes. Finally they get back in their cars and drive away confident that we are going to follow their directions, but we aren't yet convinced we need to abandon the idea of the jungle path.

There is a farm in the location where we expect the jungle path to be. An elderly lady working on one of the fields is close enough for us to call our to her. "Sawadee ka," I yell and signal for her to come over. She ignores us. I wonder if she can hear us so I yell louder. She steals a glance. Luke waves dramatically making himself obvious. Finally she stands up straight and looks us in the eye. There is a wave of confusion or possibly fear flooding her face. She shakes her head and walks into a nearby shed. Well that didn't work! I notice that a young girl has come out of the farm house and is standing watching us. We call to her. She refuses to come close to us but listens to our questions. I'm not sure if she just doesn't understand us, knows there is no jungle path or doesn't want us entering her land to get to the path. In any instance, she keeps pointing down the road saying, "Sai Yok."

"Kop kun ka," we thank her and start walking down the road. "Looks like we are going to have to follow this road instead," Luke says.

"Yeah, I don't think we can take these dotted lines indicating there is a 'jungle path' at face value. Just because the map says there is a path doesn't actually always mean a path exists."

"It's going to add a few kilometres to our walk today. But I'd rather do that than search for hours for a path not there and have to take the road anyway. Or maybe to find it, but get lost 'cause it's completely overgrown or something."

The rain has made the day much cooler than normal. This means we can walk for much longer between breaks. Gone are the days of walking for twenty minutes maximum and then resting for ten minutes. We can walk for a good hour or so before we need a rest but other issues arise when it rains. My feet are saturated through which isn't good for my skin or blisters, but we power on and find that today is a bearable day.

No major issues, injuries or mistakes, except for my encounter with a monster.

Silently walking behind Luke, I hear a quiet growl behind me. Turning, I barely have time to think as a filthy, ferocious dog bolts towards me with mouth wide open, pointed teeth and evil eyes.

I start screaming, "No, no, no, NO, NO, NO!" I wave the map I'm holding praying for my life but waiting for the dog to latch itself onto one of my limbs. It's utterly terrifying. My heart is thumping, my eyes are open wide and my mind is assessing the situation. At the very last minute, I take a step towards the dog. It's a brave move and it is my only hope. It works. It freaks the dog and he cowers, running away from me as quickly as he had advanced. It's a stark reminder that we have to be wary of the dogs here in Thailand. They are not our friends.

When we arrive in Sai Yok we make our way straight to the temple. We talk to an old monk who obviously doesn't speak English and is completely stumped as to why two *farang* are standing before him. He makes an announcement across the wat grounds via an overhead speaker system. Next thing hordes of monks emerge from the distance and one sole monk who, we soon discover speaks English, approaches us. In fact, he speaks English very well. It doesn't matter though because he is still confused as to what we want. "You want hotel?"

"No, we would like to sleep at the wat. We have a tent. We can put it up anywhere on your grounds. We don't need anything else."

Finally it dawns on him. "Oh! Here!? You want to sleep here? Okay!" Feeling refreshed after a bucket bath and some food, we settle into our tent at the usual time of 7.30pm and fall asleep.

∞ ∞

This wat has about forty resident roosters and chickens. Ever since we arrived, the roosters have been chasing the chickens around attempting to mount each and every one. The chickens have been very distressed and trying with all their might to escape the roosters defiling them. Therefore, it was a noisy night and a distressing morning as we woke to the roosters crowing from 4am and listened to them attack every chicken in sight from daylight.

When I do emerge from the tent, I find that the world has been covered in a low lying mist. We are truly in the mountains now. The mist creates a cool and moist atmosphere. It doesn't take us long to pack up and get walking. We don't even see the monks. They have left for their collection of alms already and we leave before they arrive back. I hope they know our gratitude.

Soon after we start walking, the mist begins to rise, not by much though. The fairy floss-like clouds just hover above the crops. I wish I could run my hand through it and lick sugary goodness off my fingers. Instead, I'm left craving sweet things; lollies that will make my teeth go rotten and cakes covered in chocolate icing that will satisfy my yearns. My thoughts of candy and cake are broken by a Thai man on a motorbike who has pulled up beside us. "Kao?" he says. Luke and I look at each other. We get so much attention on the highway and I'm starting to feel nervous about these people that approach us. I can tell Luke is feeling the same way and we both decline the man's offer for food. He doesn't speak English. He doesn't know who we are and he wants us to go with him. I don't trust him. For the first time on this trip we have questioned a local's intentions. "I think we did the right thing," I say.

"Yeah, I didn't feel comfortable going with him."

We are proved wrong about half an hour later when the same man pulls up beside us on his motorbike, proudly extending his arm with a bag of bananas in his hand suspended in mid air. Maybe we should have trusted him? He simply wanted to give us some food. He so desperately wanted to give us food, he went and bought some and sought us out! In the modern world we are taught to question everyone. From childhood we are told, 'Don't talk to strangers', 'Don't take food from strangers!' We lose an innocence that, if still held, would allow us to experience so much more in life. It is because of a few *bad* people that we have to teach our children and ourselves not to trust. This journey through Thailand is challenging the worldview I have always held. I am being encouraged to believe in another human being, in people whom I do not know. I am being challenged to trust in the unknown. It's uncomfortable. It doesn't feel normal or even right. I feel like I'm being naughty. Like, if my mother knew what we were doing ...

It's crazy.

But that is the world we live in.

I love that at this moment in time I am immersed in a

world where I feel I can trust those around me. It's helping me to look at the world through new eyes, different eyes, eyes filled with hope. Mr Banana Man has taught me a lesson this morning.

I'm even more thankful for the bananas when we stop for a break and instead of munching on dry noodles we have fresh fruit. These days I'm not taking anything for granted, whether it is food, shade, water, shelter for sleeping. All those essentials of life have become things we have to intentionally seek out. We can't just get food out of a fridge, or water out of a tap, and we can't go home to our house. We have to rely on ourselves or on the generosity of strangers. I like it.

∞ ∞

Walking is really taking its toll on us. I feel the need for a proper meal. We have been passing cute little roadside stalls all day and I'm tempted to suggest to Luke that we stop for something to eat.

Passing yet another, I turn to Luke, "Want to stop here for some proper food?"

"Oooo yeah that sounds good."

Originally when we were planning this expedition we had discussed only eating as the POWs had, or hadn't, as it was for them. We had researched the exact measurements of rice they had eaten and had almost made the commitment to follow that. POWs had averaged 660 grams of rice a day. If they were lucky some days they got 500 grams of vegetables, 150 grams meat and 5 grams salt.

I've thought about this often as I walk. I now know,

having walked in these conditions, that there is no way we would have succeeded in following those measurements. How the POWs walked day and night with such small amounts of food in their stomachs is a miracle. The days we have started walking without eating have really tested my endurance. The lunches, when we have only munched on noodles, have left me weak for the rest of the day. Every meal we have been given by a local I have appreciated. No matter how much we eat though, we use it all up in energy by walking. It's never long till we need to eat again.

As we sit down at a roadside stall, my belly rumbles at the prospect of some real food. Having recently learned the Thai for fried rice – *kao pad* – I'm excited when I say it to the chef and she understands me. I notice that sitting on the table there are some unique homemade fly catchers – wooden sticks covered in a green sticky goo perched in empty coke bottles. On each of the catchers are hundreds of dead flies but there is also still about a billion of the big iridescent blue pests buzzing around our heads. Even as an Australian, nothing can prepare you for these Thai flies. They are relentless and annoyingly, never-ending in numbers.

The food arrives. It's scrumptious and just what I needed. I feel re-energised and ready to go again. It's amazing what a bit of food can do for you. Back on the road we realise a storm is approaching. Luke stays behind so that he can get some photos of the phenomenon. It's times like these I'm glad I'm not a camera person. I've developed a new appreciation for film and documentary makers. It's not an easy job by any means. I've come to hate that camera of Luke's. So has he. Difference is I can walk away from it. It's a bit like when you baby sit other people's children. It's fun for a while but then you're always happy to hand them back over to Mum and Dad and return home child free. I'm willing to do some videoing but I'm aware that not only am I not very good at it, I'm even worse at initiating it myself. I generally wait for Luke to give the camera to me. It's selfish, I know. I can say to myself, 'The camera is *Luke's thing* I'll leave it to him'. Meanwhile Luke is struggling more and more each day, frustrated by the camera, the heat and me.

So, I walk on ahead leaving Luke to risk the pending storm and torrential rain it will bring. He manages to grab some incredible photos and we meet up further down the road. After an hour or so, we come to a small town. It is at this town where we are able to turn off the highway and head into the countryside again for a while. Before we do that though, we decide to ask if there is internet in town. I highly doubt it, but it's worth a try. Finding the phrase for 'internet cafe', Luke goes to ask a local. I stand back thinking this is ridiculous. As if they are going to know what we are talking about.

"Ráan nét?" Luke asks.

The guy calmly points down the road. I can't believe it! There is an actual internet cafe here? We walk five shops down – lo and behold – there is a proper internet cafe with about twenty computers. Not only that, there is ... scoop ice-cream, Luke's weakness. It's not just any ice-cream either; a cup laced with cornflakes, chocolate ice-cream, strawberry ice-cream, strawberry topping and a wafer. It's heavenly. For the next two hours we update our website, write blogs, post photos and get in contact with our loved ones. As I lick the delectable ice-cream and watch the rain fall outside, I'm grateful for the modern conveniences that have infiltrated this small town. Currently I'm in heaven. Ice-cream and contact with the outside world have lifted my spirits. It's just what we needed.

11

What do you think about?

"There is nothing either good or bad but thinking makes it so."
William Shakespeare

I love how the rain in Thailand teems down so hard and intense that all life in its path must seek shelter. Then a mere half hour later the sun comes back out and people reemerge to continue going about their day. Everything in sight dries up so quickly in the fierce Thai sun that it's as if it never rained at all. Before you know it, sweat is once again streaking your face and the rain is but a distant memory.

Our visit to the internet cafe was our shelter from the latest bout of tropical storm, but now we are back on the road continuing to cover our distance for today. We have left the highway and walking through rural land once again. I'm overcome with wonder at the scene before me. The crops of tapioca and papaya exude a sweet essence that arouses my senses. My mouth waters and my nostrils flare at the aromatic breeze I'm walking through. Dotted throughout the farms are rubber plantations, and the aroma of rubber soon overtakes the sweetness of the tapioca and papaya. Crossing the River

Kwai, which we are still seeing along the way, I stop on the bridge to take it all in. Magnificent yet slightly imposing mountains are the backdrop to the picture of a gently flowing river that sparkles in the sunlight. As I walk past more farm houses, I'm envious that this landscape is the daily sight for these privileged rural Thai folk. I bet they don't even know how good they have got it. At times, even I am taking these surroundings for granted. Therefore I'm doing my best to consciously take in what I'm walking through. I want to remember these mountains and what it felt like to be surrounded by them. It is these moments when I realise just how incredibly blessed I am to be here.

Lost amongst the simple houses of a small farming village is Wat Num Kui. The monks, as usual, are surprised to see us, confused as to what we want and, eventually, delighted to have us stay. "Norn lup ... wat?"

"Sleep? Ahhh hotel!" replies a confused monk.

"No ... wat!"

"Oh sleep wat?! Okay!"

Having stayed in quite a few temples now we have learned that some temples are better than others. This temple is lovely in all respects; the wash room is clean, the temple is well-kept and the monks cook us dinner even though they will not be eating again till sunrise. In fact, I'm blown away that the monks have decided to *cook* us dinner. This is a first for us and I'm thrilled to have fried rice and fish for dinner.

Today, for the first time, I realise just how much I stink. A sweet and sickly smell radiates from my t-shirt. When having a wash I notice that my travel towel has the imprint of a brown hand on it – that's *disgusting*. We have avoided civilisation for most of this trip so far, but being in the internet cafe today made me very self-conscious. I'm filthy and I stink. I hadn't expected to wash much at all on this walk, yet so far we have been given these daily opportunities to bucket bath. Even so, we are still looking and smelling pretty awful. Every day when I soap myself the skin tingles all over. For those few moments I'm reminded of what it feels like to be clean. The downfall is that I wear the same clothes every day, just giving them a quick wash when I bathe myself and put them back on wet. I guess it's not surprising I smell. The daily bucket bath is simply washing me and my clothing enough to keep the stench bearable.

Taking advantage of free time and mobile signal, we call our parents tonight. Our parents are very supportive of our crazy antics, yet I know they worry, especially mum, and a phone call is the least we can do to ease her mind. It's great to have a chat and tell them all the exciting things we have been experiencing.

Mum asks us an interesting question, "So what do you think about when you're walking?" The question has really made me think! It's true that we have hours of walking each and every day. There must be things running through my head.

Luke and I chat about it after the phone call and realise that for the first week, when we were walking along the railway, we talked a lot of the time. We were excited! We spent so much time discussing our route and talking about what we were seeing and experiencing that there wasn't much time left to think. When we did have time to think, it was the heat that was on our mind and how unbelievably hard it was to walk under the harsh Thai sun. So that was the answer for the first week of walking.

Week two has brought different conditions to walk in, cooler and a change in surroundings. Luke and I have been talking less which has meant more time to think. We have found ourselves walking in silence for hours, sometimes, all day. A big difference, now we are walking on the highway rather than walking on the railway line, is that on the highway we tend to walk at different paces. Often there is a good one to two hundred metres between us. To be honest, I've often looked at Luke walking ahead of me and wondered what he might be thinking. So, as Luke and I settle into our tent, I lie and ponder – what have I been thinking about whilst walking?

I spend a lot of time thinking about Tom, my new husband whom I miss terribly. I worry about how he is coping without me. I know he doesn't do well by himself. We differ hugely in that respect. As an introvert, I'm content spending time alone, in fact, I search out time alone. Tom is the opposite. As an extrovert he needs people around him all the time. Alone time makes him uncomfortable and too much of it can have a negative effect on him. I have managed to talk to him most days on the mobile but nothing compares to being with someone in the flesh.

I think about my relationships with my family, especially my brothers, seeing as I'm spending an intense month with one of them at the moment. Luke and I have always been good friends. But like Tom, Luke and I differ greatly. To look at us from afar you may be mistaken that we are alike – we are both adventurous, risk takers, love travel, enjoy making people laugh – but when you look closer, you realise that we approach all these things very differently. This expedition is testing our relationship. Every day is bringing new stresses and more tiredness. The danger of having hours and hours of thinking time each day means I can mull over little things. They can quickly become big things in my mind, like when Luke says something to me (what did he *really* mean by that) or he reacts to me (did I do something to upset him?). Honestly, it is these thoughts that are driving me insane.

I think about Thailand and how much I love it. Having lived here during 2007-2009, Thailand is a special place for me. I am loving every moment of being back in this country. Interacting with the people, eating the food, taking in the sights – it's incredible. I'd love to live in Thailand again. This trip has opened my eyes to a side of Thailand I hadn't seen before; the real Thailand. It's better than I could have imagined.

I also spend a lot of time thinking about how I love what I'm doing. I'm living a dream! I'm doing exactly what I want to do. I'm exactly where I want to be. I wish this could be my life, forever. But I'm also aware that I'm married and with that comes compromise and sacrifice. I know that Thailand isn't Tom's first choice of country to live in. Thankfully I also know deep down, that no matter how much I love what I'm doing on this expedition, I love Tom more than all of it. I hope this won't be the one and only expedition of my life. Therefore, I think a lot about doing this type of thing again but next time with Tom by my side.

My thoughts are broken by Luke's quiet voice, "Are you

still awake Rachel?"

"Yeah."

"I just realised we are half way through the walk."

"Oh ... Wow ..." I say and then remain silent. A million thoughts are running through my mind and I'm trying to process what Luke has just revealed.

"How do you feel about that?" Luke finally asks, breaking the silence. How do I feel about that? It makes me want to cry. Already I can feel the emotion building and tears racing to my eyes. I try and keep a steady voice. "I feel sad. I feel like it's coming to an end already. Before we know it, it will be over and I'll be wanting to be back here."

"Really?" Luke sounds surprised. "I feel like there is so much more to come!"

"How do you mean?"

"Well, for the first half of the expedition we knew what to expect. We knew we would follow the railway track and visit museums in Kanchanaburi and Hell Fire Pass. But the second part of the walk we are much more unsure of."

"Yeah, I guess you're right ..." This is proof that Luke and I approach the same things ... differently.

"We don't have maps for most of it! Only the dam section, and we still don't even know what the dam section will be like."

"Oh yeah! And that last fifty kilometres to Sangkhla Buri, we have no map at all!" I suddenly remember.

"Exactly! There is so much more to come Rachel."

Wow, it is interesting to hear how different our perspectives are on things. Luke's glass is half full. It seems mine is half empty. I need to change my attitude. I remember back in Bangkok I was so scared. I had no idea what to expect or if we'd even be okay. But now that we are half way through, I recognise that there is a confidence inside me that wasn't there at the beginning. I feel secure and optimistic about what is ahead. Even if things get tougher in this second half of the expedition, I have faith that we will work it out, together.

There are some moments in life when you step outside yourself, take a look around and realise you are 100% happy. This is one of those moments.

I fall asleep to the soothing sound of croaking frogs and singing cicadas. The noises of the jungle are loud and continuous. It is a constant reminder that I am in a foreign place. I'm miles away from home but the sounds of the jungle, the jungle that symbolises beauty, solitude and overcoming adversity, comfort me.

12

A Tiny Speck of Gold

"You gain strength, courage and confidence
by every experience in which
you really stop to look fear in the face ...
You must do the thing which you think you cannot do."
Eleanor Roosevelt

"Please! Luke! Turn around!"

I've hit the wall. I'm broken. I don't want to walk anymore – but Luke is about one kilometre ahead of me and no matter how loud I yell, he can't hear me. No matter how much I will him to turn around so I can wave my arms for him to stop, he isn't turning around. He is on a mission to just keep walking. With no motivation or determination this morning, I have slipped well behind Luke. We are back on the highway and it's a living hell. I hate it. I want to stop. I *need* to stop.

"LUKE!" Nothing, he just keeps walking.

"LUUUUUUUUUUUUUKE!"

Damn it! Why won't he turn around? Before I know it, the tears have arrived and I'm crying, moaning; I'm a blubbering mess. I'm so tired. I'm so sore. I'm sick of walking! I'm fed up with carrying this heavy backpack. I'm over the heat. "Please *turn around!* I need to *stop* Luke. I *can't* walk *anymore!*" I'm delirious, screaming like a mad woman who has lost control of her mind and reality.

It is so hot today; unbelievably, infuriatingly, irrevocably *HOT.* Back in Kanchanaburi, I purchased a fan for 50B; best purchase of my life. This fan has been a life saver; it's an ever constant breeze that I carry around with me. Today I'm using it more than ever. I'm afraid I'm developing RSI (repetitive strain injury) in my wrist. The only rest it gets is when I walk in the shade and I take this time to give my shoulders a break by taking the backpack straps off and holding them in my hands for a few metres.

Finally Luke sits down on the side of the road to wait for me. I don't let on how much I've been struggling. I simply say, "I really needed a rest," when I catch up to him.

His reply is, "Yeah, I just had to keep walking 'cause if I stopped I was afraid I'd never get going again." I guess I'm not the only one finding it tough.

I've been reminded of something this morning. The POWs also walked through conditions like these but at the mercy of their cruel captors. They could only stop when they were told they could stop. The Japanese were relentless in their wickedness and would make the POWs march for hours and hours before they would allow a rest stop. I've wrestled with my emotions this morning, being in the hands of Luke. He was in front, therefore, controlled our pace. Yet no matter how hard I have found this morning, it bears no comparison to the POWs. Once again I have reverence for the men who trod this path many years before me and endured pure hell.

I came on this trip to have an adventure. I knew that

to seek adventure would require something of me; it would put me to the test. I think I've been yearning to be tested, to discover I have what it takes. Today is testing me beyond what I ever thought I would have been capable of.

To make matters worse, we are no longer using a 1:50,000 scale map. These maps showed villages coming up, wats along the way and terrain. Now we are using a 1:250,000 scale map that was printed in 1985 – 26 years ago – it's completely useless. So we have to just keep walking and walking. We have no idea what is ahead. How far is it till the next town – no idea. Is there a wat in the next town – no idea. Will we be passing any form of civilisation in the next few hours – NO IDEA!

I'm still keeping that tally of the number of people who are stopping to help us. The most so far, before today, has been six offers of a lift. Today is turning out to be the winner though. So far we have had eight people stop and another has just pulled over. The air-conditioned car is shooting out an icy breeze that is calling my name. We have said no to all eight offers today. Are we actually going to say 'no' to this one too? We have no idea how far we need to walk to the next wat. We keep asking people who stop, "Glai mai wat?" and their answer is always, "Wat?! GLAI!!!"

The lady speaks English and her offer is extremely tempting. "I think that you come in the car with me to Sangkhla Buri 'cause I go to Sangkhla Buri."

"Ohhh, thank you but no. We have been walking for two weeks! We are following the footsteps of the prisoners of war from World War Two. We are walking to Sangkhla Buri!"

"Ah okay!" the lady exclaims, "Yes I see you on the highway so I turn around and come back two kilometres to pick you up 'cause I think you go to Sangkhla Buri so you come with me."

"Well, we are going to Sangkhla Buri but we will walk ..." I can't believe we are turning this offer down. The lady is very sweet, accepts our explanation and bids us farewell. "Ok then, well good luck with your trip!"

Every time a car stops we ask how far it is to the wat. The problem is we keep getting quoted different distances — 1km, 3km — there is a big difference between those two when you have to walk it and you have already walked twenty kilometres.

Another car stops and the man is eager to give us a lift. We decide to try and ask if we can stay at his house, but his English isn't that good and he doesn't understand what we are trying to ask. We keep telling him we *want* to walk. He keeps saying, "Ok, well it's up to you!" If only he could understand that we want to stay at his house! We can't get the message across so the kind man drives away and we ... keep walking.

Further up the road a teenage girl is standing by the road watching us. As we approach she waves and walks toward us.

"Where you going?" she asks.

"We are going to the wat," Luke replies.

"Which wat? Wat Thong Pha Phum or Wat Prang Ka Si?"

"The closest one!" Luke and I cry in desperation.

"Oh, Wat Prang Ka Si."

"Glai mai? How far?"

"Um, two kilometres. Ah, do you want to come with me, I drive!" She points to her motorbike.

"We have been walking for two weeks and we want to walk." We sadly decline yet another lift.

Nodding she says, "Okay." She then extends her arms out holding a plastic bag with two ice cold bottles of water. I've never been so ecstatic at the sight of cold water. The water really hits the spot. As it slides down my gullet I can feel chilled liquid filling every corner and crevice of my insides.

"She must have seen us walking, gone and bought these water bottles, then come to offer us a lift," I say to Luke.

"I know hey, it's so awesome."

Finally, in the distance, a tiny speck of gold peaks above the tree line. It's the spire atop the red roof of a wat. I want to sprint towards it but I'm completely wrecked, gone, obliterated. Even now with the temple in sight I can only walk as fast as my legs allow me.

We enter the temple grounds to find that there are monks ... everywhere! Flecks of orange are dotted around the place and every one of them is pretty much ignoring us. It's a bit strange. We find a group of boy monks sitting with an elder monk. This elder monk speaks English.

"We would like to sleep at the wat?" I ask.

"Oh, down at the river?" he replies.

A bit confused I try and clarify by saying, "Shelter?"

"Yes, down by the river!" He tells two of the boy monks to go with us.

Next thing we know we are walking *away* from the wat down a jungle path to a river. It's only a five hundred metre walk but after today it's absolute torture. We end up at the river standing looking down a steep bank while the boy monks point to the river and smile. Getting eaten by mosquitoes and envisaging a night in the jungle, Luke and I flatly refuse to follow their instructions. Using the phrase book we find the word for bridge. The boy monks nod. Then we find the word for roof.

"No, no," they reply.

"I don't think there is shelter down there Rachel," Luke says.

Finding the word *better* in the phrase book, I say to the boy monks, "Norn lup, wat, deegwah."

They understand: sleeping at the wat is better. "Okay," they reply and lead us back to the path.

On the way back they point to a shrine. Though it is a shelter, there is no way I'm sleeping in that. The mosquitoes down here are frightfully abundant and obviously hungry for a feed. Using the phrase book, I'm able to communicate to them that I want them to ask the elder monk for a shelter we can use, "Tahm poochai." Simply saying 'Ask man' in Thai has helped. They whip out a mobile phone and give the man a call. Normally I would have found this funny, but at the moment I don't care that this boy monk is holding a mobile phone. Finally the boys say, "Lungkah, yes, yes!" It seems they are saying we can have a roof but I'll believe it when I see it.

When I eventually do see it, I don't believe it! It is a brand spanking new wooden cabin – fit for a honeymooning couple on one of Thailand's famous islands! Still under construction the only thing it's waiting on is power. It's absolutely perfect. I don't understand why the monk had us walking down into the depths of a mosquito lair when there was an empty cabin available all along. Who cares, we are here.

"Yee um!" I say to the boys telling them it is excellent. They walk away grinning, giggling and bubbling over with joy. I wish I could say the same for myself. But rather, I'm hot … bothered … exhausted.

∞ ∞

This wat is creeping me out; the insects are piercing the night air with their high pitched squeals; the monks have stayed up late into the night calling their bone chilling chants which seem to be floating into the cabin and remaining suspended in mid air right above our tent; and so far in the cabin I've seen a spider the size of my hand, millions of mosquitoes and there are packs of dogs patrolling the temple grounds. To add to the eerie atmosphere, I just woke up to an animal *inside* the cabin. I could hear its nails scratching along the wooden floors. I lay very *very* still as it walked around the cabin for a while then departed. It could have been anything – a tiger or an elephant – though most likely a dog. Doesn't matter, I don't trust any of them out here! I'm conscious of the adrenalin pumping through my body and know that if I get any sleep tonight, it'll be a miracle.

As I try and fall asleep I find myself immersed in a dream – whether it is real or not I am unsure …

I am wandering through the jungle. It is dark but the moonlight creates a path that leads me to the river. On the other side of the river, I can see people standing on the bank. Though their faces are blurred, I know that I have met these people before. I wish I could reach them but the current of the river is too strong. Standing beside me is the Warrior of Light.

"Why can I not reach them?" I ask.

"It is not yet time," the Warrior of Light replies.

"It is my desire to be with them. To stand by their side."

"Child, you have much to be thankful for. You are free to choose your desires and to make your own decisions with courage and hope."

Frustrated I reply, "Yet I am in pain. How can I know whether my decisions are the right ones?"

"Remember that yesterday's pain is today's strength. You must take every opportunity to teach yourself. And you must have faith."

"I hear you Warrior of Light. But know this: I will only risk my heart for something that is worthwhile."

The Warrior of Light smiles.

13

Blue Paper Snowflakes

"Love your neighbour as you love yourself."
Romans 13:9

In Thailand there is a small, unassuming plant which, though small in size, displays a fascinating characteristic; it has sensitive leaves that snap shut in an instant when brushed against by grass, animals or a human hand. The leaves recoil, curl up and close themselves off to the outside world.

I fear this is where Luke is at right now, ready to recoil, curl up and close himself off. Yesterday I was in pain and struggled with inner turmoil but it seems today Luke is the one struggling. Not getting a decent sleep at the wat the night before has not helped matters. We were both glad to get out of there this morning. I don't think either of us even turned back to watch it fade into the distance. The vulnerability of sleeping so close to unidentified creatures had been a little unnerving.

We have stopped by the side of the road for a five minute rest. I'm waiting for Luke to say he is ready to go. Silence has meant the rest has turned into a half hour one. Waiting patiently, grateful for the long break, I quietly amuse myself by touching the sensitive plants and watching their leaves draw back as though I am something to be feared.

After a few hours of walking, we come to a junction in the highway. We have been following the 323 highway this whole time but now we are turning onto the 3272 highway. I stand for a moment at the junction looking into the distance of the 323. There is a sign pointing that way which says, 'Three Pagoda Pass' – the Burma border. This is the first indication we have had that we are anywhere near the end of our journey. If we continued following the 323 we would be at the border soon, but we are choosing to follow the 3272 highway as it is the closest we can get to where the original Death Railway stood. We will meet up again with the 323 in a few days.

Along the 323 highway we have often used the bus stops as rest points. They are quite large platforms with benches and a roof. The sight of them always makes my heart skip a beat at the promise of shade and a chance to take my backpack off. Many a time, we have confused bus drivers who think we are waiting for a bus. Having become accustomed to the honk of a horn to grab our attention, we now shoo a bus away before it even has the chance to try and pick us up. I'm positive that the bus drivers are becoming familiar with us. Some of them would be travelling up and down the highway on a daily basis. For the past couple of weeks they would have seen two *farang* walking north on it. I'm starting to suspect that many of the honks we get from the buses are the drivers saying, 'Hello, I've seen you before!'

At the junction of the 323 and 3272, there is yet another bus stop. Luke begs for us to have another rest there and I don't complain. We both take our backpacks off and take a seat on the benches. Luke is soon lying down on the bench. I'm a bit worried as he seems to be really struggling and I'm not sure what I can do to help. In no time it is obvious that Luke is asleep. Now I really don't know what to do. Should I wake him? He must really need the sleep, so I just sit and wait.

Forty minutes later Luke wakes suddenly as though forced out of a deep sleep and an even deeper dream. "How long have I been asleep?" he asks, bleary eyed.

"About forty minutes," I reply.

"Wow, I'm really, really tired."

We start walking again and two hundred metres down the road we discover there is a roadside food stall. We don't even ask each other; we both just walk over, take up a plastic chair and collapse our heads on the table. Using my ever growing Thai, I order *kao* (rice) and *neu a moo* (pork). I'm learning more of the Thai language on this trip than I did when I lived here for a year and a half! We sit for a long time talking lazily about many things, avoiding the inevitable. We are both dreading going back out into the heat. The sun's rays are hammering through the heavy, humid air and there is no breeze to take the edge off the burning sensation. I've taken my shoes off and put a needle through yet another set of blisters. My feet are in dire need of a couple of days' rest. Our goal for today is to make it to Thong Pha Phum, the town near the dam, and to find a place to stay for two days. We are in desperate need of a break from being on our feet.

We know that once we make it to Tha Ka Nun, we are close to the dam. We decide to ask the lady at the food stall. When she puts up two fingers I'm shocked. Two kilometres? We are much closer than we thought! Re-entering the punishing rays of the sun, we start walking and soon make it to Tha Ka Nun. Asking some local men how far the dam is, they reply that it is five kilometres.

"We can do it," I try and remain positive.

"Yep, let's just keep walking," Luke replies.

"Our aim is the wat, right? Try and ask if we can stay for two nights?" It hasn't taken us long to abandon traditional hotels, motels or any other form of paid tourism accommodation. I'm confident we will find a kind stranger who will take us in, even if the temple doesn't want us.

∞ ∞

The past two kilometres have been complete agony. It must be at least 40°c; the sun is oppressively hot; there is no wind; and the sweat is running into my eyes, burning them. Through my sweat-burnt eyes, I notice a small sign that says iPraise Church. At first, I have a giggle that even out here the Apple brand has influenced the culture. Secondly, I think that this might be a great place to try and stay. We have slept at Buddhist temples this whole journey. It is time we get back to our roots (both Luke and I being Christians) and experience a church in Thailand.

Although we are heading in the direction of the sign, finding the church proves difficult. With the help of locals, eventually we approach a pale pink building that looks nothing like a traditional church.

Standing out the front is a man. "Hello," he says, when he sees us.

"Sawadee ka," I still use the Thai greeting despite

his English one.

"Come in." I think our exhaustion is obvious.

"Do you come from the church?" I ask. The man nods.

"Do you speak English?"

"Yes."

Relieved that we will be able to explain ourselves in a language we will both understand, we sit down and tell him our story. "We have been walking for a very long time. We started walking from Ban Pong in Kanchanaburi; we followed the railway to Nam Tok; then we walked to Hell Fire Pass, Sai Yok and now we are here."

"Okay," he simply replies.

"We are following the footsteps of the prisoners of war from WWII," I add hoping he will know what I am talking about.

"I see. Is this personal or for an association?" he asks.

I'm surprised by the question. His English is very good it seems.

"We knew someone who was a POW during the war. We walk in memory of those who built the Thai-Burma railway," Luke answers.

"Ok, personal," the man clarifies. "Did your friend die here?" I leave Luke to answer as he was closest to Stan, "No, after the war he returned to Australia and he died two years ago."

"Are you also Australian?"

"Yes."

"Ok."

Taking a deep breath, I nervously add, "So while we have walked, we have been staying at the wats and at people's homes. We saw your church sign on the road and came to see if we could stay here at the church as we are looking for somewhere to rest before we set out again."

The man calmly replies, "It's okay, yes, you can stay."

"Would it be okay if we stayed for two nights?" I ask, but feel like I'm asking too much. "Two nights?" he says. Now I'm worried we are pushing his kindness too far. "Yes, we would leave Sunday morning."

"You can stay two nights," he says, then adds, "Why don't you join us for the Sunday morning church service?"

Uh oh, I'm anxious about committing to something like that when I know we have to get an early start the day we leave. "What time is your service?"

"10am."

"Um, ok ..."

"If we go too long you can leave," the man adds, sensing our hesitation. "Right ok, well maybe, we shall see."

The man stands up, extends his hand to ours and says, "My name is Surathin. I will go and prepare for you."

Luke and I look at each other. I'm positive we are thinking the same thing, 'Have we done the right thing?'

Sipping on the ice cold water that has been brought for us, we wait patiently. Five minutes later Surathin comes back with two young girls, his daughters. The girls walk us through the first floor of the building, which is a cafe, and up the stairs to the second floor, which is the church hall, all the way up to the third floor which we soon realise is their house. It's an incredibly simple house and an untidy one as well. We meet the pastor's wife (by this stage we have discerned that Surathin is the pastor of iPraise Church) who is scurrying around in a bedroom tidying up, making the bed, sweeping and getting the girls to remove belongings from the room. Luke and I stand awkwardly in the corner not sure what to do with ourselves. Unfortunately for Luke, the pastor's wife is only wearing a silk gown which is very precariously balanced, slipping off and inappropriately exposing a bit too much, causing Luke to find the ceiling incredibly interesting.

I divert my eyes as well by taking a closer look at the room we are standing in. It's quite a large room. There is a double bed; a wardrobe that is spilling over with clothes; and a lot, and I mean *a lot*, of soft toys. In fact, there is a lot of stuff. In many ways, I feel like I'm standing in the storage room of a charity store, but it dawns on me whose room this actually is: the kids. They are kicking their children out of their own room and giving it to us. Where are the kids going to sleep? Now I feel really bad! We never meant for them to give us their very bed.

The girls and their mother leave us to settle in, not before making sure we know how the air-conditioning works. Luke and I lay on the bed, enjoying the air-con and not saying a word. Suddenly the door swings open and one of the girls is juggling a water jug and some plastic cups. Trying to open the door with her foot has not worked and the cups go crashing to the floor. She giggles as I jump up to help her. Noticing that she didn't knock on the door I make a mental note to always remain decent as surprise entries, I imagine, are going to be common. We are quite a novelty for the girls; they keep opening the door just a crack and then giggling uncontrollably.

I leave Luke to rest, and step outside the bedroom to explore the house. There isn't much to explore; one other bedroom, a bathroom (with a shower!) and an area of the house I guess you could call the laundry which has a fridge, a washing machine and a floor strewn with rubbish. I decide to take a shower and wash my clothes. Washing my clothes for the first time in clear water, I discover just how filthy my clothes are. The water turns brown, no matter how many times I wash the clothes in fresh water. It's clear my clothes are in desperate need of a proper wash. They won't be getting that for a while. When I leave the bathroom I notice something I had missed before. Sitting in the foyer is a large, gorgeous, wooden swing seat fit for a prim and proper English garden. This place is full of surprises.

The cafe downstairs is run by the pastor's wife and we decide to support the church by eating dinner here. Speaking very little English, the pastor's wife makes us feel welcome and even gives us an extra dish to go along with the Tom Yum soup we order. It is a rice dish covered in vegetables and seafood. The squid is so soft and delicious, I want to cry. For dessert we both have a large strawberry sundae. We are treating ourselves tonight – we need it!

I watch the family as they eat together. I can tell now why their house is so simple. They basically live downstairs. They eat down here, work down here and the kids hang out down here. Surathin comes over and invites us to the prayer service at 7.30pm. We are exhausted but knowing we aren't planning to stay for the Sunday Service, decide we should show our face at the prayer service. It's the least we can do for all they are doing for us.

The church hall is very small. There are twenty blue

plastic chairs facing a slightly raised platform. Surrounding us on the walls are banners in English and in Thai – Holy is the Lord, Praise the Lord etc. On the platform is a cross made out of gold piping and wrapped in fake maple leaves. Draped from the ceiling is red and gold material and blue paper snowflakes hanging on string.

The service begins with Surathin playing guitar and singing whilst using a lapel microphone with headset. The set up is like a mega church except that there are nine of us here and we are all a maximum three metres away from him. In the front row, the pastor's wife is singing loudly and proudly into a microphone as well. Shame she is completely out of key. Singing goes for an hour. The small congregation are loving it, singing majestically and raising their hands to the sky. Most of the songs sung are written by Hillsong (a mega church in Sydney, Australia).

I'm kind of disappointed that church in Thailand is almost no different to church back at home. It seems that their expression of faith is a hybrid of the *western way* and the *Thai way*, resulting in a disparate mix of customs. I wonder what the Thai church would look like if it expressed its faith through its own culture.

Luke whispers to me, "I think we should leave now, before they begin the talk so that we aren't leaving during it." I agree. I'm completely and utterly exhausted. I won't last through a talk anyhow. We sneak out and retreat to our bedroom. We fall asleep in an instant.

14

Finding Comfort in the Chaos

*"One of the most valuable roles music plays is to
build the reservoir of our memories.
It serves as a rewind button that brings back the
past in a fond remembrance.
In that sense, it helps connect life's dreams to
life's accomplishments."
Ravi K. Zacharias*

Downtown Thong Pha Phum is a bustling market place early in the morning. Stalls selling clothing and household goods fill the square, and motorbikes weave in and out of local people going about their daily business.

Luke and I are drawn to a character-filled food stall where pork and chicken hang on hooks and people slowly eat whilst bent over, engrossed in deep conversation with a friend. The man in charge juggles the organised chaos with ease; he seems to know who everyone is, what every one wants and never needs to ask twice. He walks over to us and announces we can have, "Pork or chicken!" Lifting up lids of massive pots, he shows us boiling broth filled to the brim with tender looking meats. My mouth is watering so much I ignore the fact that hanging above the pot is a dead chicken staring me in the eye.

Both of us choose pork, which arrives with rice and is doused in gravy. It's so delicious, I devour it in minutes.

I notice that sitting at the front of the food stall is a man making black sesame wraps. I recognise these treats, because a monk gave us some a few days ago. Savoury in taste, crunchy in texture, the cylinder shape reminds me of a perfectly rolled crepe. It's fascinating to see how these are made. Onto three small waffle maker type machines, he squeezes batter from a bottle and then shuts the lids. When cooked, he peels off the round pancake-looking creation and rolls it onto a small wooden tube leaving it to set hard. It's already a hot morning and I spot that the chef is sweating profusely. I can see the droplets of sweat falling straight into the batter. It doesn't end there either. He then wipes his forehead with his hand and continues handling the wraps. I have no doubt that this batch will have a hint of sweat amongst its flavour; extra salt!

After a rest back in our room, we decide to venture out into the town again to find internet. The pastor's children follow us out the door and into the town. Smiling and giggling, they eye us off as they walk beside us. Clueless as to where to find internet, after a few wrong turns we ask the children, "Internet?" They come to life and run ahead calling us to follow. Soon we are sitting in an internet cafe, sipping a coke and thanking the heavens these children can't read English. Hovering like a bad smell over our shoulders, they are entranced by the screen. They eventually get bored and leave.

On our arrival back at the house, we discover that our bags have been gone through, most likely by the children of the household. It's not overly obvious but what gives it away is Listerine soap sheets scattered all over the floor. Listerine soap sheets are a new*ish* product – they feel and look like a small piece of paper, 2x2cm, but are actually soap which froths up when used with water. Great for travelling. I pick one up and laugh out loud. One of the kids thought it was a lolly and there are some definite teeth marks in this particular sheet. "That's what you get for going through other people's things," I say out loud to no-one in particular.

I take the opportunity for the rest of the afternoon to lie on our big double bed and listen to music. I don't have an iPod with me as I couldn't justify bringing such a luxury, but I do have a wind up radio. Radio has influenced the way the world listens to music and hears local and world news.

Radio was extremely important for the POWs who worked on the Death Railway. Secret radios were hidden in broom heads, shoes and other every day items (in fact, I saw some of these secret radios in the museums in Kanchanaburi and Hell Fire Pass). Radio was how the prisoners learned what was actually going on in the war. They would secretly meet together to listen. It was a haven from their everyday hell. When secret meetings weren't possible, one person would listen and report back to the group. When they didn't have radio, they put on theatre shows and organised sing-songs. Music was a big part of what kept the POWs sane.

I remember Stan talking about the songs that got him through his three years as a prisoner. *I need thee* is one particular hymn that he held close to his heart. For Luke's documentary, Stan and his wife sang the chorus of *Pack Up Your Troubles*, a

WWI marching song. The words say it all.

Pack up your troubles in your old kit-bag,
And smile, smile, smile,
While you've a Lucifer to light your fag,
Smile, boys, that's the style.
What's the use of worrying?
It never was worthwhile, so
Pack up your troubles in your old kit-bag,
And smile, smile, smile.

When I think about it, I realise that on this journey I have been missing music immensely. Only since removing music from my life have I realised how much music is a part of me. All I have access to is Thai radio but I'm not complaining. Thai music is spicy; it is filled with different textures and hair-raising tempos. Luke is not impressed with the Thai music with its shrill melodies and high pitched cries. I admit, it isn't music that calms the soul but rather strains the ear drums. Nevertheless, I need music. Music is so important – music triggers memories. The simple melody of a song can remind us of a first kiss, a long lost best friend or, for some, the news that changed their life forever. Music is used in rehabilitation, nursing people back to good health; music can be used in celebration or used during a mourning process. Music is a part of life.

As I lie and listen to the unsettling sounds of the Thai music emanating from the radio, I'm quietly satisfied that this music, for the moment, *will* give me the desired effect. It will calm my soul. I have no doubt that when I hear the sounds of Thailand in the future, it will transport me back to moment like this, when I sought solace in the music of the land.

∞ ∞

I have been talking to Tom everyday on the mobile. Thanks to Skype, we can afford to do so. It's been great to hear his voice each day and to share the adventures I've been having. But today's conversation isn't as positive as previous days. I've been missing home today and as I relay this to Tom, he is very silent. When I finish my rant, I ask him why he is so quiet.

His response hurts to hear, "Well, I'm not in a good place myself to be helping you. I'm in the busiest and most stressful time of my uni life. I'm getting ready to say goodbye to London and move to Australia. My days are so boring; all I have is uni work and no friends are around."

This breaks my heart. Have I been selfish in coming on this expedition so soon after we got married, let alone months before we move to Australia! I don't know how to respond to what he has said. Say sorry? Sorry for going away and leaving you alone in a time you need me the most. Say thank you? Thank you for allowing me to come on this expedition despite the fact we both knew it would put strain on our new marriage. I don't say either of these things because I honestly don't know what to say to make things better. We finish the phone conversation on a pretty negative note. I'm in tears – I'm across the world in a country I love, doing what I love and all I want is to be with the one I love. But that can't happen. I'm literally stuck in the middle of Thailand and it is weeks till I can see Tom again.

I go back to the room and talk to Luke about it all. At least I'm not completely alone. I could be doing this expedition by myself, but instead I have someone by my side. I'm thankful for that. It's good to vent to Luke, to ask the questions that taunt me everyday but that no-one can answer. Luke listens quietly and allows me to debrief my phone call with Tom. Luke asks, "So how were things left?" Truthfully … I don't feel that we left things in a good place at all.

I decide to call Tom back. When I say hello he says, "I was just thinking about calling you back! I saw the photo of you that you put in my letter and it made me laugh." Before I left I put together a little pack for Tom, filled with envelopes he was instructed to open only on the date stated on the front. Each envelope was filled with a letter and a small gift. Recently he had opened one of the envelopes to find a photo of me he had taken on our holiday in Switzerland the year before. I'm trying to put a raincoat on and look like a real idiot. But it's one of Tom's favourite photos of me. We talk for another ten minutes. It's all good stuff. We leave the phone call this time in good spirits.

I think about the song Stan sang, *Pack up your troubles in your old kit bag and smile, smile, smile.* I picture Tom, and imagine the moment when we will be reunited. And I smile. At this time, being apart is not easy, but I have faith that it will only make our relationship stronger.

∞ ∞

It's the 15th May, which means, it is Luke's birthday. He is turning twenty six years old today. I can't believe he is so old! I still feel like I'm twenty six, yet my thirtieth is looming at the end of this year. Meanwhile Luke, to me, is still a fifteen year old running around jumping off roofs. I think he still feels like this too. Unbeknown to him, I have been carrying around a birthday present for him. I set my alarm a little earlier so that I can get up before Luke and set the camera up to video our little birthday exchange.

"Happy Birthday Luke," I whisper as loudly as I can. Luke's eyes open. At first he looks lost like a little child searching for his mother in a crowded shopping centre. Then he realises we are alone in a room in Thailand and it's his birthday.

"Oh wow!" he says when he sees me holding out a small but grand present to him. "I really didn't expect this!" He didn't expect this? What! I couldn't let his birthday go by without making something special of it! He opens his present to find a KidRobot, a party hat and a small packet of lollies.

The KidRobot is a new craze in London. They are small figurines that hang off a clip. Luke's is a little angel and he attaches it to his trousers.

He holds up the lollies, "I'm excited about eating these!"

It's a small affair but I hope that the little surprise has helped it to feel like his birthday. Today is a big day. Besides being Luke's birthday, we are reaching the dam wall today and we have no idea how it's going to turn out. With only the one gift to open, we move on to packing and preparing to leave.

Ready and rearing, we step outside the bedroom to find that the house is silent. Not wanting to disturb the family, we regretfully decide we need to leave. Our departure proves difficult as the downstairs is completely locked and we can't get out of the building! It was a mistake to think that the family would be up early. We heard them crashing around the house at 2am! We had wanted to tell the pastor yesterday we were planning to leave early but interaction with him had been minimal during this stay.

We hang around for half an hour, but when no-one emerges from the pastor's bedroom by 7am we decide we have no alternative but to knock on their door.

Luke and I whisper in the darkness, "You knock."

"No, you knock!" etc.

Finally one of us knocks and the pastor's wife comes to the door, "We're terribly sorry we need to go. Is it unlocked downstairs?" I ask. With no English she stares blankly then walks back into the room.

Seconds later the pastor is with us, "You are leaving?" he says as he walks past us into the bathroom.

"Um, sorry yes ..."

What now passes are two incredibly awkward minutes while Luke and I stand outside the bathroom listening to the pastor's powerful morning pee ritual. It's so loud and so awkward that Luke and I look each other in the eye and start to giggle. Trying to compose ourselves is difficult.

When he emerges he simply says, "I will unlock for you."

The pastor leads us downstairs and unlocks the gate for us. Wanting him to know just how grateful we are for having been given a room in their house, I try and express my gratitude with words.

"Thank you so much for letting us stay and for welcoming us into your home."

The pastor keeps his normal emotionless expression, shakes our hands and walks back into the building. He doesn't say a word. As we walk away from the pale pink church I ponder how this family had welcomed us yet had been uninvolved with us; how the pastor had been kind yet withdrawn. It had been a different couple of days.

15

No Admittance

*"If I'd observed all the rules
I'd never have gotten anywhere."*
Marilyn Monroe

I've seen it in my dreams, on our topographical map and on Google maps, but today ... I will stand on Vajiralarjkorn Dam wall. Luke and I have studied the surrounding land, zoomed in on the terrain and explored this area for hours on Google maps. This is the part of the walk that we have researched the most, but now that we are actually walking towards it, we are still clueless as to whether we will be able to cross the dam wall. Crossing the dam wall should allow us to follow the shoreline for a kilometre or two, taking us to a road we can see on our map that heads away from the dam through small villages.

It's a coolish morning and as we are approaching the dam we come across a toll booth.

"Just keep walking, act like we know what we are doing," says Luke.

Eyes forward, I don't even turn when the guard (who

has a gun) calls out to us, "Excuuuse me!"

"Keep going!" Luke whispers. But the guard is determined and runs up to us.

"Excuse me! Car?" he says pointing to a jeep. That I did not expect, to be offered a lift. We decline, leave the man standing puzzled, and continue to walk the further three kilometres to the dam.

An anticipatory flash of excitement fills Luke's face when we finally see the dam wall in the distance. I can sense my face is also lit up with the buzz of delight I feel at the sight of this monstrous man-made structure. Over the past two weeks, Luke and I have spent hours discussing our arrival at the wall, and now, we are here! It's an incredible feeling but that feeling is quashed when I take note of just how *monstrous* the wall is. Spanning across the horizon, the wall has to be at least one kilometre long, if not two. I'd always imagined we would just walk to the end of the wall and go over the side. I'm now not so sure. I'm questioning whether we will even be allowed near the wall.

"This is going to be interesting ..." Luke mutters.

The Dali Lama says, "Learn the rules so you know how to break them properly". Unfortunately we have no idea what the rules of the dam wall are, but I have a feeling we will be trying to break them.

We can see another toll booth ahead of us but it's obvious that this is for employees only. We decide to try and get past anyway, trying the tactic of 'We know what we are doing", again. It fails. We haven't even got close when a guard sees us and points up another road. I hadn't noticed this road which is also going towards the dam wall. When we reach the end of this road we come to what seems to be a tourist centre; a quaint, well kept, lush green garden with an unusual souvenir shop selling hand painted wooden peacocks, and a brand new toilet block. There are even Thai tourists wandering around the centre, having picnic lunches in the garden and more tourists can be seen up on the dam wall taking photos of each other. Of all the things we had imagined, the dam wall being a tourist attraction was not one of them. This is a problem. Tourism brings people, and rules; people attract attention that we don't want and rules are something we might not be able to heed if we want to cross this wall. How are we ever going to discreetly get to the other side of the dam wall?

It's really hot, as usual. Taking a rest, Luke munches on his lollies I gave him this morning, and I utilise the clean toilets. We are essentially avoiding the inevitable. Finding the motivation to put our backpacks on and climb the stairs to the top of the dam wall, we make a move. It's not a long walk but it's a tough one – I'm hot, sweaty and nervous. I have no idea what to expect.

Reaching the top, I'm surprised to find that the view is staggeringly beautiful. The dam water is the iridescent colour of a peacock's blue neck; painted on the horizon are resplendent mountain ranges with emerald green trees; the sky blue heavens are cloudless and flocks of birds are flying in their perfect V shape into the distance. I stop to take it all in. I want to remember this moment forever. I take a photo with my camera but know that the real image of this will stay imprinted in my mind as long as I live.

Coming back to reality I take a look at what we are facing – a steep dam wall and a lack of shoreline. However, we are determined to get to the other side. We decide to walk along the dam wall but half way come across a sign that says, 'NO ADMITTANCE.' It's even in English. For the first time ever on this trip we decide to do something we *know* we are not suppose to do – we walk past the sign. It doesn't take long at all before a guard on a motorbike is driving up to us. He speaks in Thai, pointing at the sign and shaking his head; we know exactly what he is saying: 'You're not allowed here.' I'm quietly freaking out. What is it about a human in a uniform that causes one's knees to wobble and heart to palpitate? It may seem ridiculous, but both Luke and I know we must get to the other side. Not following the planned route along the dam, turning back and going on the highway again is, for us, not an option.

The dam is a part of the Death Railway story. Therefore, it is of great interest to us. Construction of the dam began in 1979 and took five years to complete. The dam was originally called Khao Laem Dam but was renamed after Crown Prince Maha Vajiralargkorn. The Prince is the only son of the current and much loved King of Thailand Bhumibol Adulyadej. Due to the *lèse majesté law* (the crime of violating majesty) the Prince cannot be spoken of critically, but everyone knows he is not well liked, unlike his father who is revered by many Thais and has reigned in Thailand since 1946. Vajiralargkorn Dam holds a strong connection with the Death Railway because the dam now sits over a forty kilometre section of the original Thai-Burma Railway route. In fact, the two ends of the railway were joined at Konkuita on October 16, 1943. Konkuita now sits under Vajiralargkorn Dam. So I don't care how long we have to stand here, I'm making sure that this guard understands what we want and assists us in some way. I'll stand here all day if I have to. The problem is the guard doesn't speak English. I can see the road we want. It is about two kilometres along the shore of the dam. The road leads to a village called Ban Thung Samo.

"Ban Thung Samo?" I say, pointing in the direction of the road. The man nods eagerly. "Dern?" Asking in my limited Thai about 'walking' seems to work. The man understands but he is also shaking his head. We cannot walk there. I keep trying, "Dern?" and pointing at the non-existent shoreline of the dam. The guard continues to shake his head.

"What about a boat," Luke suggests. Here we are again asking for a boat, but it seems it might be the only way we can get there. "Reu-a?" I ask.

The man nods. He then rambles a long sentence in Thai, and looking at our map, he points to a village on the mainland called Ban Tha Phae about five kilometres away. I'm not entirely sure, but I gather what he might be saying is that if we go to this village, we can get a boat to take us to the road we want. I'm frustrated. I can see the road we want from here. Why can't a boat come here and pick us up? I don't want to have to walk three kilometres back to the highway and then a further five kilometres to this village. That will take up most of our day! It's times like these that you realise walking really does take a long time.

The man walks away, into his office and gets on the phone. "Who is he talking to?" Luke wonders. The man is on the phone for about five minutes.

When he returns, I try and ask again for a boat, "Reu-a?"

The man nods, talks in Thai and smiles. I'm not quite sure what is going on. Is a boat coming for us? I hope so.

Soon a ute arrives with more guards inside. This time I'm not afraid of the uniformed men as it has dawned on me that the guard called up his friends to take us in their vehicle to the nearby village so we can get a boat. I'm very grateful for the man's help, and I'm not saying no to a lift this time. What an adventure this is turning out to be! Luke and I jump in the back of the ute and fly down the highway with the wind blowing in our faces. We feel free – the comfort and ease of a vehicle is not taken for granted at all! This morning we have proved to ourselves we will do whatever it takes for us to complete this journey.

At the village we are directed to a man who speaks a bit of English. He has a boat and will take us to Ban Thung Samo for 800B. I try my normal haggling skills of dropping it by half.

"Nooooooo," I cry "400B!" The entire group of people who are standing watching the negotiation fall into fits of laughter, including the man we are trying to haggle with. Have I said something wrong? "Noo! 800B" he confirms. I don't know what to do, I have no idea how much a journey like this should cost. I know that I don't want to be paying 800B though. Luke is just as clueless as I am, but we also know we don't have any other choice.

"We have to get a boat Rachel, otherwise we are heading back to the highway."

Under the inquisitive eyes of villagers, I manage to negotiate the man down to 700B. As we load our bags and ourselves into the longboat, I wonder if we have just been ripped off. The entire village is standing on the bank of the dam to farewell us. I wave to them, loving the moment. I feel like a true adventurer, a foreign body in a foreign land, exploring. The man who is driving the boat is silent not saying a word to us. He stops for fuel and Luke notices that he pays 500B for the petrol. Whether we paid the appropriate price for our boat ride doesn't matter anymore as I'm immersed in my own thoughts of adventure, exploration, new experiences and dreams coming true. This expedition is meeting all of these things, all my expectations and exceeding them by miles.

The boat ride is calm and as we float across the dam's tranquil waters, we spot fishermen in boats who wave at us as we pass by. The sun's rays are shimmering off their aluminium dinghies and I can see their buckets filled to the brim with fish jumping and flapping around. Forty five minutes later we are dropped off at the road that leads to Ban Thung Samo. We can see the dam wall and it's hard to believe we were standing on that a mere hour ago. The man helps us to dismount the boat and make our way onto the steep, muddy bank. He waves to us as he drives away and suddenly I feel very alone. I'm not sure I've ever felt so much like I'm in the middle of nowhere, stranded, away from the real world, as I do now. I've just allowed myself to be abandoned on the side of a dam. No one knows where we are and I don't even really know where we are going. As I slip and slide up the muddy bank, I say a prayer, "Please God, keep us safe."

I smile. They stare. I say, "Sawadee ka!" They stare. Three small children are standing on the path as we leave the dam behind and I have a feeling they have never seen a *farang* before in their lives. They are expressionless; they don't smile, talk or move. They just stare at us.

"Don't think they get many tourists around this joint!" I joke to Luke.

On the shore of the dam is a small village and it is noticeably different to all the others we have come across so far on this trip. The houses are built on stilts, made of bamboo and are as simple as you find. The way these houses are spread out amongst the trees makes me feel as though I am an adventurer entering the grounds of a tribal land. Then, I realise that is exactly what I am. This is what it looks like to live out my dream! It's currently over 40°c and I'm sweating profusely but I don't care. I'm in a remote village in Thailand and I'm exactly where I want to be. Today I'll take the heat in my stride.

16

In the Middle of Nowhere

*"I would rather wake up in the middle of nowhere
than in any city on earth."*
Steve McQueen

It's immediately obvious that people are surprised to
see us. Even the adults, sitting on the bamboo balconies of the
houses, are staring at us with blank looks. I'm not quite sure
how to take their reactions or lack thereof. I can only hope we
aren't upsetting anyone by walking through their village. We
call out a friendly, "Sawadee ka!" as we pass through.

At the end of the village we find a track and are
immediately immersed in thick jungle. It has all the
characteristics of a jungle too: stifling humidity, increased
temperature and millions of mosquitoes. We stop on the track
to have something to eat but find that as soon as we stand still
hundreds of mosquitoes tuck into their lunch too – us. I walk
up and down the track to keep moving, swatting my legs and
arms, whilst trying to eat dried noodles. People using the track
to move from village to village pass us and offer a friendly,
"Sawadee!" accompanied with the Thai wai. I love the wai –
with hands in a prayer-like pose against the chest, one bows as
he/she greets someone. It's the traditional Thai sign of respect

and it's used by everyone. The older the person you greet, the higher the wai is on your body. Monks who deserve the utmost respect receive wais that sit on people's foreheads.

The afternoon is tough going and we are glad we have no choice but to stop walking at Ban Thung Sao after seven kilometres. It is the only village we will come to today and it is our only option for sleeping tonight. I'm not sure what constitutes a village out here in the remote areas but we have just walked passed a small group of houses and I have a feeling that it might have been the village. Turning back, we ask an old man sitting on his bamboo porch, "Ban Thung Sao?" He nods.

"Oh, this is it!" Luke says looking around at the few houses, "Where are we going to sleep tonight …?"

"Um yeah … no idea," I add. The man gestures for us to come onto the small porch.

"Maybe here?" Luke asks.

"Worth a try!"

Luke and I make ourselves comfortable on the porch. With our shoes off and backpacks resting on the ground, we are grateful to be able to sit down. It doesn't take long for more people to come over to the porch; a lady and two young guys are peering at us with interest.

No one is saying anything, so to break the awkward silence I attempt to ask about sleeping at this house. "Norn lup?"

I get blank looks from everyone. I try a few more times but am getting nowhere. It seems odd. I've never had this much trouble before. It's like these people don't speak Thai. Then it hits me like a surge of monsoonal rain – they don't speak Thai!

I look up the word for Burmese. "Pah-mah?" I ask.

They come alive, nodding and saying, "Pa-mah! Pa-mah!"

So these are the Burmese we have heard so much about. In fact, we have been warned about their being illegal and possibly untrustworthy. Patrick in particular, at our very first wat, warned against Karen and Mon tribes. I feel very different, even a little uncomfortable, knowing we are now amongst Burmese people.

I take a closer look at the people we are sitting with. It's obvious now that these people are Burmese. They look different to the Thai people, darker skin and broader noses. Even the atmosphere amongst them is different; the usual friendliness and kind nature we have experienced in the company of Thai people is not felt here with these Burmese that live deep in the Thai jungle. A noticeable difference is that all the men are chewing betel nut; what teeth they have left are stained red. The nut they chew is actually called Areca nut. The name Betel comes from betel leaves that they wrap the nut in along with slaked lime paste, to chew. The old man stands up and goes inside. I assume he has gone to get us a drink or possibly something to eat. He comes back with a small wooden box. The bottom of the box is lined with betel leaves and a small tray that sits in the top has a silver container of lime paste and a nut cutter. The old man offers us some of his precious betel nut. It's kind of him but declining this offer is not hard when he shows us his toothless crimson grin.

After another ten minutes of trying to communicate through sign language alone, they finally seem to understand that we want to sleep somewhere. But we aren't being invited to sleep at their place. They keep saying, "Wat!" and pointing down the track. The group of Burmese talk incessantly to each other. Meanwhile, we have no idea what they are saying but we are sure they are talking about us. An old man we haven't seen yet walks up to the balcony we are sitting on. He is jabbering away in Burmese at us as though we can understand him. We can't. He shakes Luke's hand then grabs my hand. The handshake is firm and he lingers just a little too long. He then proceeds to stand and stare at me. I feel extremely uncomfortable.

"Luke, I don't like this old guy. His eyes are lingering on me," I say through closed teeth trying to keep a calm face to show no hint of concern.

"Oh, yes I see what you mean," Luke replies through gritted teeth.

Suddenly the group comes alive and seems to want us to follow this disturbing old man. Everyone is indicating we can stay at his place, I think. But I know that there is no way I am going anywhere with him.

"Let's go and try to find this wat they have been talking about," Luke suggests.

We stand up to leave, saying thank you and hoping we won't upset anyone. It's so hard when you can't speak the language or read expressions. We are offered a ride on a motorbike but we decide it's time to leave these Burmese people. As we farewell the group and walk away, the old man seems to think we are going to his house. He keeps pointing in the opposite direction and nodding as if to say, "Yes, you can come to my house. This way!"

Luke and I keep walking and walking. Every time we

turn around the man is still there behind us, following. I feel anxious. We are in the middle of nowhere with a disturbing old Burmese man following us.

After five hundred metres Luke says, "If he is still following us after this bend I'm going to go back and talk to him." Thankfully after the next bend the man has given up and turned back home.

It's been a strange afternoon, a strange day. My brain is finding it hard to comprehend that this morning I was standing on the dam wall surrounded by a flash tourist attraction and I'm ending the day leaving a village where simple, rural people live. The contrast between the modern and the remote ways of life in Thailand is astonishing.

I'd assumed the wat wouldn't be far away, but we keep walking and walking. No wat appears. Passing two guys along the path, we ask them about the wat. They point ahead of us. I'm very confused and starting to question whether there is a wat, despite the fact everyone is telling us there is. Then it starts to rain. Our rain ponchos get another use and as we walk further and further into the jungle, no wat comes into sight. The rain has brought grey clouds and everything is becoming dark. Desperate to find somewhere to sleep, I start to panic.

"Luke, we haven't seen people in a while. Where are we going to sleep?" Looking around it's obvious there is no way we are going to be able to camp. The jungle is dense, impenetrable and uninviting. The rain is making everything wet and muddy. My fear of sleeping inside a tent that simply floats away on a river of rain water during the night, is becoming a horrible possibility. "We are just going to have to keep walking I guess," Luke says.

I don't want to sleep in the jungle. I don't want to get eaten by mosquitoes. I don't want to be saturated through. Tonight, however, I may not have any other choice but to sleep in such conditions. It sounds a lot like the reality of the POWs. Suddenly we hear the dull throttle of a motorbike as it races passed us on a path up ahead. Luke and I look at each other then run, not wanting to lose sight of it. A motorbike means people and maybe even a house. Puffed and sweating underneath our plastic ponchos we are led by the motorbike to an incredible sight.

Hidden amongst the thriving jungle is a house so stunning, so splendid yet so simple. Built on stilts, it towers above the jungle floor as if to say, '*I am* the king of the jungle'. What astounds me the most is that out here in the middle of nowhere is a place where people live, a place they call home. These people are standing outside curiously watching the two *farang* approach their house. There are six of them and I can't decide yet whether they are suspicious of us or intrigued. First things first, I establish whether they are Thai or Burmese. They are Thai. We show them our map which they are fascinated by. The locals always are. I guess they have never seen a 1:50,000 scale topographical map of their land.

Attempting to build good relations with them, I decide to try a new phrase I recently taught myself, "Norn lup tee bahn koon?" This translates to *sleep at your place?* Obviously impressed by my Thai, they giggle to each other and nod in affirmation. It seems they are more than willing for us to stay. I'm more than relieved. I feel like this family has saved our lives! We probably would not have died spending a night in the jungle, but I didn't want to find out.

After climbing the rickety bamboo ladder to the house built on stilts, we are shown a platform where we can set up our tent/mosquito net. The rest of the family will sleep in the one room that constitutes their kitchen and bedroom. The tall bamboo house is surrounded by banana trees and rubber plantation. Looking at the surroundings, I see the family owns rubber trees and must make decent money as they even have a satellite sitting on their roof. The entire set up of this family's life is simple and yet it is perfect. Even their outdoor toilet has character with potato sacks for a door.

We sit down with the family and try to determine with them where we are on the map. We are not sure we know where we are anymore. We are also wondering which way we will need to go tomorrow morning.

Pointing to the path on the map and the jungle path that backs onto their property, I ask if the road is good, "Tanon dee?"

Nods all around.

I point to a village I can see on the map further north, "Ban Khanun Khli?"

Nods all around. It seems that the road we need to follow tomorrow is the one that passes by their house. Maybe we aren't as lost as we thought we were.

The family consists mainly of young adults and one elderly lady. A girl indicates to us about having a wash. We are shown an outdoor water bucket. The bucket is huge and stands as tall as myself. It is filled to the brim with water and there is a small plastic bowl to aid in pouring water over your body. Luke washes first. When it comes to my turn, I'm not sure it would be culturally appropriate to wash in my underwear, but I don't have a sarong, so I wash in my clothes. Later I see the family wash and the girls wear sarongs. I wish I'd asked them for one. It would have been a much better wash. Regretting my shyness in asking for a sarong, I resign myself to the fact that instead I looked like an ignorant *farang*.

The same girl who showed us where to wash brings us some food. It is four peculiar bananas. They are really thick in diameter and have a pink skin. She also gives us some strange savoury jam biscuits and strawberry juice. The girl says something in Thai to us as she goes to leave. I'm not entirely sure what she has said but guess she was saying, 'Don't come out of the tent. I'll bring the food to you', so I simply smile in return. Grateful for the snacks, we tuck in while we wait for what we assume is our dinner being cooked in the kitchen. Safe inside the tent, away from the hungry mosquitoes, Luke and I talk lazily about many things. It doesn't take long till I'm enthralled by Luke's stories. Luke has always been a good story teller. Whether fact or fiction, he can relay a story in such a way that makes it feel real. I never get the feeling of 'Oh, you had to be there,' as I'm always in stitches when he is telling a funny tale. His stories always take a long time to tell but are always worth the wait. Today he is telling me about a documentary he watched about the 'Out of Africa' evolutionary theory. The idea is that modern day humans stem from a single group of Homo Sapiens who emigrated out of Africa 150,000-200,000 years ago and spread out over Eurasia. It's fascinating. I'm so absorbed by the stories, theories and pictures Luke is creating that I forget we are waiting for food. We both suddenly realise it is quite late.

"Maybe we aren't getting more food?" I suggest.

Luke chuckles, "Maybe what the girl actually said to us when she gave us the bananas and stuff was that this was all they would be able to give us." That makes a lot of sense when I think about it.

So Luke and I venture out of the tent to cook ourselves some noodles. We even treat ourselves to some freeze dried mash potato and peas. It is Luke's birthday after all.

17

Lost

"I may not have gone where I intended to go,
but I think I have ended up where I intended to be."
Douglas Adams

I wake to the most incredible reality. White cloud mist is hovering so low that if I stood in it only my ankles would show; birds are singing, insects are calling and gibbon monkeys are honking in the distance. I feel completely isolated but this remoteness from the rest of the world is a welcomed feeling.

The family we stayed with overnight has been up for hours already. They were straight to work on their rubber plantation and as I sit on the balcony I watch them, intrigued. The guy is arriving back on his motorbike with a big blue bucket flled with fresh rubber. He has just come from collecting rubber from *tapped* rubber trees. When a rubber tree is tapped, a slit in the trees bark is cut which causes a wound to bleed. The sap that bleeds runs down the tree into a cup the size of half a coconut, attached to the trunk. Every month or so the cup is emptied into this big blue bucket and brought back to the house. The sap from the tree is rubber in its liquid form but if you pick it up in your fingers, you find it is a stretchy substance. The guy passes the bucket to his sisters who then proceed to drain the rubber through a sieve into another bucket. This removes any dirt, insects or other impurities. Meanwhile, another girl is working on rubber that had been put into rectangle trays on a previous day. This rubber has now set and she is slapping each sheet on the floor and rolling it out, like you might do to dough. These bath mat sized rubber sheets are then hung up to dry on a line. It is these sheets that they sell. I've seen rubber sheets hanging up like this in all the rural areas of Thailand we have passed through. I find the sight of these white sheets hanging, lined up like soldiers, mesmerising.

Thailand is the world's leading producer of rubber. According to the Thai Rubber Association, in 2010 Thailand produced 1,504,261 tonnes and exported 1,316,237 tonnes. In June 2011 the price for rubber was between 130 – 150B per kilogram ($4 – 4.68). Rubber is an industry that can make people a lot of money. In a country where a bottle of water will cost you 5B and a long distance train journey 25B, I'm not surprised so many rural Thai families own rubber plantations.

It's time to go. As I look around I know that sleeping at this house that is so remote, unadorned, charming and secret, has been a definite highlight of the expedition. Back in the *real* world whenever I get stressed or anxious, I will transport myself back to this place where life is simple and the burdens of the outside world are overshadowed by the flourishing and ever changing jungle.

As soon as we start walking, we realise we are in for a

tough one. The dirt path has, with all the rain, turned into mud; the motorbikes that use these paths daily have destroyed it so much that really it can no longer be called a path; our shoes sink and stick in the mud; climbing over the troughs created by the bikes is a work out; and it's all at a 45° angle so we keep sliding backwards. It's also at least forty degrees with one hundred per cent humidity, but we plod on, mumbling silently to ourselves about our inner struggles.

It doesn't take us long to realise that despite our conversation with the family yesterday, we really are not sure where we are on the map. There are no landmarks, no houses or lakes, no way of determining our position on the map. We keep walking in the hope we are heading in the right direction. We haven't seen people all morning. Luke and I haven't spoken in hours. I'm simply enjoying walking through this remote part of Thailand. Even if we are lost, I don't mind. I have faith that everything will be okay.

Arriving at a crossroads causes a little bit of concern but as we stand on the junction trying to decide whether to continue straight or take the right turn, two ladies straddling a motorbike come down the path. It's a miracle. We ask them where Ban Wang Khayou is, the next village we expect to pass through. They point to the right turn. It's a good thing we were able to ask someone for directions as I'm pretty sure we were about to continue on straight ahead which would have resulted in a major detour.

The mountains we are climbing today are beautiful. Conquering them is calling for every ounce of strength within me but the views at the top are worth all the hard work. From the top we can see to the horizon and there is no civilisation in sight for miles, just land that looks strikingly like a painted mural. Despite the seemingly barren land, we have started to pass a house here and there. Farm houses that dot the path, separated by their neighbours land, are very isolated. One man calls out to us and we walk over to say hello. He is wearing a pair of shorts only and his bare chest shows the signs of years in the sun. He takes a grubby glass and fills it with water from a large dirty bucket. Smiling at us proudly he stays to watch us gulp his precious water. With no other option, Luke and I both guzzle the glass of water, closing our eyes so we won't see the grimy finger prints on the glass and blocking our minds so we won't panic about what impurities this water might be carrying. When you are in the middle of nowhere and a kind stranger offers you a glass of water, you just can't say no. I wish we could stop and get to know all these people we are meeting along the way. Too often we have had to give up the opportunity for new friendships and new experiences. It's actually a really difficult thing to do.

I feel like my life is a cycle of learning one particular lesson: life is about people. Money, power, materialism and status are not important. I came on this trip to be tested, physically, mentally and spiritually, but quite unexpectedly, now that we are over half way through the walk, I'm beginning to see the expedition in a different way – not as an endurance test but as a test in relationships.

My relationship with my husband has been tested. The distance and inability to see each other or talk properly means we are forced to work harder at our relationship than ever before. If we can make it through this time I'd like to believe we will make it through any other test that comes our way.

My relationship with my brother has been tested. Luke and I are two very different people. I haven't lived in Australia for nearly four years and in that time both of us have changed. We are no longer the kids who play games, climb trees and cause mischief (to be honest, it was Luke causing all the mischief). We are now both grown adults; we come with a bucket load of experiences from our past which have made us who we are today. Some of those experiences were good, some were not so good. I feel that Luke and I have realised on this trip that we maybe don't know each other as well as we used to. This has meant we have to work hard at learning how to be in each other's presence on such an intense level. We have to try and work together, in harsh conditions, while trying to keep the peace. It's been a challenge. Sometimes the silences between us have been intentional and ... awkward. At other times, we have talked deeply and shared stories of our past, present and future. We've snapped at each other and yet at other times we have encouraged each other.

We choose every other relationship in our lives but we don't choose our family. Family is a constant. Luke will always be my brother and because of that I believe we will make it through anything.

The tensions that have arisen between us during the expedition have caused me to look deep within myself. In the real world, I'm free to be who I am and not acknowledge that there may be parts of me that need to change. Living and working so closely with someone who is not only a friend but my family has caused me some pain. I've recognised characteristics of myself I'm not proud of.

The question is, now that I'm aware of the things I *want* to change about myself, am I *ready* to commit to the reality of looking even more deeply within to make those changes? I don't have an answer yet. All I know is that I feel a little bit lost; the Rachel that arrived in Thailand is not the Rachel I want to leave Thailand. I want to be a better person.

∞ ∞

"Where are we?!" Luke says, exasperated at our reality. We are lost.

"I'm so confused. Everyone we have passed, we have asked about Ban Wang Khayou and they have all pointed the way we are walking. I don't understand why we haven't come across it yet. According to the map it should be here! I think we must have come out a bit higher than I expected. So I think we need to turn right onto this road and walk south for a bit," I reply.

We are standing on a main road. Having walked through the remoteness for two days, it's a little confronting being faced with civilisation.

A young guy walks passed us, so I ask, "Ban Wang Khayou … glai mai?" His answer surprises me. He points *left* up the main road and says *fifteen* kilometres. I figure I've misunderstood him so I ask the same question of the next person who passes by. I get the same reply.

So here we are, lost and unable to speak Thai, aside from a few words. We walk further down the road and approach a lady who is standing outside a house. It's practically impossible to communicate with her. People start to notice that we are around and come over to suss things out. We end up with a large group of people around us, all talking *about* us and rarely talking *to* us. It looks like they are arguing about which way we need to go. Luke and I give up, say thank you and taking the previous advice we have been given to start walking north. Then the rain comes. Big, fat, heavy droplets of rain come hurtling towards earth. Luke and I run to a shop shelter, buy a cup of jelly and wait out the rain. It's gone after ten minutes. You wouldn't even know it had been raining monsoonal style just moments before. Already the sun has evaporated every droplet of water and I'm sweating profusely while my mouth cries out for a drink.

As I pull my water bottle out of the side pocket of my bag, I look up and see a sign. It has three little symbols that I never thought I would be happy to see – 323. I turn to Luke and I can tell he has seen the sign too. We are back on the wretched 323 highway that promises hours of boredom broken by moments of terror as a bus hurtles towards us on the shoulder.

Stopping to look at the map, it's embarrassing to see how badly we read our map today. And our compass! We thought we had walked directly north all day and that we would come to the village of Wang Khayou. Instead we walked directly north-east all day which led us back to the dreaded 323 highway. On the map, I can see a village called Kroeng Krawia that sits on the highway. There is also the symbol on the map for a temple in this village. I thank God that we are back onto a 1:50,000 scale map and ask someone how far it is to the village. I'm very pleased when the reply is two kilometres.

Approaching the wat, we see an old monk sitting chatting to another man. They are surrounded by boy monks who run and get us bottles of water. It seems the hospitality we have received at other wats is to be found here too. The old monk shows us where we can sleep, inside their wooden temple where the Buddha shrine will watch over us all night. As Luke and I settle into cooking our dinner, we soon find ourselves surrounded by a curious bunch. All the boy monks are watching with interest at our strange cooking contraptions.

A monk we haven't seen yet comes and introduces himself to us, "Hello, I from Burma!"

"Oh wow, that's nice," I say.

"You go Burma?" he asks.

"No, we won't be," Luke says sadly. We had talked about walking in Burma but the logistics of it was a nightmare considering the current political situation there. Stan, our ex-POW friend who is the inspiration for this expedition, hadn't gone to Burma so we didn't feel we needed to.

"I in this wat six day!" the monk declares proudly.

The monk is very friendly and studies our maps intently. He is fascinated by our journey. It's nice to have someone who can speak English so we can talk about our trip freely. The monk relays our story to the boy monks who stare at us adoringly with wide eyes. They too are fascinated by our maps and are fighting over who gets to look at them. The monk notices we are eating our noodles out of the pan.

"You need bowl?" he asks. This Burmese man seems different to the group we met in the jungle yesterday. I'm finding him more approachable and willing to assist us.

"Ok, we will have a bowl," Luke tells him.

"I have many bowl!" he cries as he scurries over to where a huge pile of bowls is stacked in the corner of the temple. I can't help but giggle – I love this part of the world.

∞ ∞

It's 8pm but I've already been in bed for half an hour. This has been the norm on the expedition. Each evening I'm completely exhausted and give myself an early night to keep myself well rested. The lights are off and the darkness is calmly pulling me into a deep slumber when suddenly a light comes on in the temple. I open my eyes and watch an old monk shuffle his way from the entrance of the temple to the shrine at the other end. Sitting himself down in front of the shrine, he proceeds to pray. When a Buddhist monk prays, it is a succession of chants sung at the one tone. It loses its enchantment when you're trying to sleep. To be honest, I wish the guy would just finish. He did, at about 9.30pm – but he returned to pray at 5am.

18

Tâm Sukow

"Once you accept the existence of God
— however you define him, however you explain your
relationship to him —
then you are caught forever with his
presence in the centre of all things.
You are also caught with the fact
that man is a creature who walks in two worlds
and traces upon the walls of his cave the wonders
and the nightmare experiences of his spiritual pilgrimage"
Morris West

During the war, monks allowed POWs to use the temple as shelter. The monks were a source of rest and kindness even all those years ago. I like the fact that sleeping in temples is another small connection we have to the POWs and their experiences. The monks of Thailand have come to mean a lot to me; they have offered me shelter, food and a greater understanding of what it is to be a human being. I've learnt more about Buddhism on this journey than I did during the two years I lived and worked in Thailand as a tour leader. As a Christian I live by the teachings of Jesus, but that doesn't mean I can't learn from the Buddhists.

The Dalai Lama tells his western students that they

don't have to become Tibetan Buddhists in order to be his pupils. I admire the Dalai Lama. He welcomes his students to take any of the ideas of Buddhism and integrate them into their own lives and religious practices. The Buddhist emphasises that, because Buddha is not a creator, no-one should just naively believe his words. Rather, Buddhism encourages people to think and analyse before they accept its beliefs. I like this. In fact, it reminds me a lot of my own faith. Christianity says 'don't believe everything the Bible says'. Test it.

The Buddhist also believes that all thoughts, feelings, emotions, unconscious and subconscious, are a river of mental moments. Everything we do, say and think leaves an imprint. Therefore we are the result of our past and the cause of our future. For the Buddhist monk this means he purposefully chooses to live a life of kindness, openness and hospitality. These same traits are also important for the Christian life. The difference for the Christian is that Jesus is our example. He taught us to love our neighbour; he always put others first. If I can lead a life that is anything like a Buddhist monk, or Jesus, I'll be happy because it'll mean that I've had a positive impact on those around me.

During Weary Dunlop's last year in captivity, Weary treated a Japanese soldier. This enemy soldier had walked to the Burmese border with a gangrenous leg and attempted to amputate the leg himself. Weary was reminded, whilst treating this man, of the Buddhist utterance that in the face of suffering all humans are equal. This is something I've gained from the monks we have encountered. They don't know who we are or why we are here, but none of that matters. We are fellow human beings in need of the simple but necessary things of life and they have been more than willing to offer that to us.

We say goodbye to yet another wat and another group of monks that have become our friends overnight. I hate saying goodbye. I just want to stay and get to know them better, but alas, we must walk. I don't expect to be walking far today, maybe fifteen kilometres or so, although, as usual in these latter days, we are not entirely sure how far it is to the next wat where we will try to stay. Today we are, in fact, walking off our map. From now on we will have no map, no indication of where we are nor of how far we have to go. This is not a huge problem as we are back on the 323 highway and we will be following this to our final destination, Sangkhla Buri. We are finding the road conditions this far north, atrocious. As another vehicle forces me to fear for my life, I cower like a frightened puppy and resign myself to the fact that our final days will be filled with chilling moments like this. We will have to drag our feet along long, straight, boring distances on this narrow road. With no shoulder to walk on, the fast cars and buses are a real concern.

After weeks of walking, my shoulders have also decided to give out. They are over it and they let me know this. The strain of carrying my heavy backpack has taken its toll and it never takes long for them to start aching. My body feels like it wants to fall apart but can't. It's like my body knows it still has a job to do and it will finish no matter what. I'm amazed at what the human body can endure. I'm also realising the price the POWs paid physically – wounds that became infected, hunger that was never satisfied and sleep deprivation that sent them mad. If my body is suffering and I'm looking after it, you can only imagine what was happening to the POWs.

The end is in sight, not with our eyes but with our minds. We are on the last stretch and it is a strange feeling. We have anticipated the bridge that leads to Sangkhla Buri for a long time. Finally, we have reached the days when we can start to talk about that approach. So far today we have walked seven kilometres to the Khao Laem National Park entry. We stop here for some lunch and talk about our options. "We know there are three wats before the bridge to Sangkhla Buri, don't we," Luke says.

"I remember one of them being at the waterfall." Pointing to a sign that says *Kroeng Krawia Waterfall* I continue, "See that sign? I reckon there is a wat around here somewhere."

"Well, in that case shall we try for the second wat? The third will be too far away I think."

"Sounds like a plan," I reply.

∞ ∞

I'm having another one of those days when I want to give up. Only the pain from my aching shoulders and blistered feet is providing the ascendancy over my temptation to fall into a blubbering mess that will no doubt result in my being curled up in the foetal position, refusing to move. While I fight the internal battle, a monk on the back of a motor bike stops beside me on the road (monks are not allowed to drive so will always have a driver). I think he is saying the name of a temple as he points straight ahead.

Luke asks, "Norn lup?" and the monk nods. The monk is extremely keen and obviously feels confident we have understood. He drives off.

"What was that about?" I ask Luke.

"Dunno, strange hey."

I think to myself that it was almost like the monk had said, 'Come to our wat! It's 5km up the road. Yes, you can sleep there. See you soon!' But it was all in Thai, so you never know for sure. More likely it's wishful thinking on my part, but Luke chimes in with, "It's almost like he was asking us to come to his wat?"

"That's what I was just thinking. Maybe the other monk from this morning talked to this monk and told him we are on our way?"

Whatever the monk said, his short and confusing encounter has lifted my spirits. I power on focusing on the promise of a wat to sleep at. A small dot appears on the horizon and coming towards us is a boy on a motorbike. He stops in front of us and I recognise the bike as the same one the monk had been on. The boy is here for us and is saying the name of the wat. He wants us to get on the bike, but much to my disappointment we have to say no. We are here to walk, but everything within me wants to say, 'YES, I will get on your bike!' The boy is incredibly confused and getting frustrated with us.

We try to explain by saying, "Dern ..."

He replies, "Dern??" shrugs his shoulders and drives away. 'Crazy farang ...' I don't hear him say it, but I know he is thinking it. He is right, we are crazy. As I continue walking on, I immediately regret our decision. It is so hot. The sun is burning me. My shoulders are killing. My feet are throbbing. I simply cannot and do not want to walk another step. I'm struggling – big time. Then the worst thing that could happen, happens. A mosquito shows up.

Bzzzzzzzzzzzzzzzz .... That sound is so irritating.

Bzzzzzzzzzzzzzzzz .... I'm seriously not in the mood.

Bzzzzzzzzzzzzzzzz ....

I start to yell at the tiny winged vampire, "FRIGGEN GET LOST!"

Bzzzzzzzzzzzzzzz ....

"GO ... AWAY!!!"

I'm not a swearer. I hate swearing. I've never wanted to swear as much as I do right now but I don't swear because that would mean the mosquito would win. I'm trying to walk, fan myself, keep from swearing and hating every single minute of it.

"I can't walk anymore," I scream to no-one. Luke is so far ahead I can't see him anymore. I feel so alone.

"I can't dooooo it!" I grapple with my inner and outer torment urging myself to continue. Tears are rolling down my cheeks, I'm breathing very deeply and I feel like I'm on the verge of collapse.

Then ... I have an epiphany.

I remember the POWs. I remember why I'm here. I remember why I'm doing this.

I tell myself, "I walk because they walked. I walk

because they walked." It's a simple sentence but it makes all the difference.

The wat is nowhere in sight. Neither is Luke. Somehow I find the strength to keep walking. Finally, I see him. Luke is up ahead and I see the boy we met before approach him and then they disappear into the jungle. It must be the wat! We've made it and I know I've said it many times before but ... I'll *never* be so glad to see a temple as I will be when I see this one. As I reach the spot where I saw Luke turn off the road, I turn myself to the right and cannot believe what I am looking at. This wat is in a cave. The entrance is tall and black, a mysterious yet inviting natural hole cut into the side of a cliff. From the road it is very unassuming; you don't even know it is there. When you stand in front of this palatial cave, an emanation of seclusion and splendour spills forth. I enter the cave.

There is something extraordinary in the atmosphere. I think Luke can sense it too. A sense of calmness and serenity wrap around me like a warm hug. I want to do nothing but stand silently and absorb the peace and tranquility. I'm also waiting for something to happen; my senses are stretched to their limits as though something out of the ordinary is about to occur. Today's challenges have pushed me to the edge, but for this moment I feel no concern whatsoever. In this moment, I am calm, hopeful and filled with faith.

The monk who met us on the road is standing inside waiting for us. He is a round monk, tubby and joyful. His smile is contagious and I grin as I take a glass of the cold orange juice he has ready for us to drink. The monks have also set up mats on the wooden platform inside the cave for us to sleep on. I feel very welcomed. The cave is spectacular. The ceiling is metres above us and the cave goes quite deep into the mountain but all I can see is blackness. Scattered throughout the body of the cave are Buddha statues, smiling, lying down, sitting, laughing, Buddhas of every kind. The cave floor is covered in blue tiles except for the wooden platform where we will be spending the night. It's an incredibly unique temple and I feel honoured, not only to be able to visit it but also to sleep in it. Something else is living in the cave – I can't see them, I can only see the evidence of them. Bat poo! That is a little unnerving I have to admit, especially when I have to dodge stepping on it in every metre of floor space.

I wander so deep into the cave that I can no longer see any light from outside. The ground and walls are damp. My movements are being swallowed up by the darkness so I retreat back to safe ground.

After spending some time in the cave, I've forgotten how hot it is. I'm slapped in the face by a wall of scalding steam when I venture back outside. There is a small shop over the road, so Luke and I decide to go and buy something to eat.

The monks see us and call out, "Kao?" Nodding, the monks wave us over to where they are sitting. An old, lanky monk with a raisin face and an exceptionally large lump on his forehead starts cooking us a meal of rice, fish in tomato sauce and pickled mustard leaves. The lumpy headed monk jabbers away to us in Thai and, with hand gestures, explains that he can't eat with us because monks only eat when the sun comes up in the morning. Having spent enough time with monks now, we know the rules and respect their lifestyle. This monk is hyperactive and bounces all over the place while we eat the meal he has cooked for us. He cooks us sooo much food but we still devour it in minutes. He then cooks more fish in tomato sauce. The monk is very animated and quite adorable. It's like watching a theatrical performance. He tells us with actions, 'You eat rice, it make you strong, you walk far!' It's amazing what you can get from a person who communicates with you entirely by actions and gestures. He also tells us, 'I was on a motorbike, I fell, now I have a bump on my head and elbow. Now I walk everywhere!'

While we are eating and talking, the tubby monk we met on the motorbike is washing. He is standing outside his small wooden hut, a bright orange robe wrapped around his waist and has soap everywhere. While he lathers himself up, he listens to our conversation. When he finishes, he comes and shows us his digital camera. There are photos of further inside the cave and I'm fascinated by the shots of deep within the mountain's belly. I can't believe we will be sleeping in a cave tonight.

We have stopped walking fairly early today and I'm thankful for the time to rest. God knows I need it. The temple grounds outside the cave are gorgeous. The monks live in small wooden cabins scattered around the place. Their bright orange robes hang from the railings and make a stunning contrast to the dark wood of the cabins. I'm sitting at the entrance to the cave, journalling and watching Luke who is inside the cave setting up his sleeping stuff. I notice he has hung his wet clothing and underwear on the wooden railing of the platform. Each day when we wash, our clothes have also been given a soak, although I'm not convinced it's cleaning them. I touch the clothes I'm wearing. They are still damp but I know it won't take much longer for them to dry.

A monk who has slipped into the cave unnoticed, approaches Luke and starts pointing at the wet underwear hanging for all to see. Luke freaks out, does a lightning turn which results in his kicking one of the glasses of orange juice with his foot and it smashes into pieces all over the wooden floor. The monk panics, afraid that Luke has sliced his foot open, and prepares to perform first aid on the spot. Luke, who seems not to be bleeding, then tries desperately to tell the monk that he is fine. While the monk stares at Luke's foot, Luke is fumbling for the Thai phrase book so that the monk will know that there is nothing to worry about. I'm still sitting at the entrance of the cave, watching all this play out. Luke finally communicates that he is okay. The monk points again and then Luke (and I) realise that the monk had in fact been pointing, not to the underwear, but to a rolled up mat that we could use. I'm grabbing my sides, rolling on the floor laughing. There's never a dull moment.

Just outside the entrance to the cave, an elderly Thai couple has arrived and is setting up a small blue tent. It seems that we aren't the only ones on a pilgrimage. The tiny wife is in control, barking orders to a whimpering husband who can't seem to do anything right. In the end the wife puts up the tent alone. The monks arrive at the cave for afternoon prayers and the elderly couple join in. Luke and I stay at the entrance of the cave and just observe. Everyone is facing the shrine, kneeling down with their hands in the prayer position. One monk takes the lead and using a microphone guides the others through a chant progression. I've got to admire their dedication and stamina. Hours later, they are still chanting when I go to bed, a mere five metres away. I'm not sure how I fall asleep, but I do.

∞ ∞

"Oh man I'm so tired," Luke says rubbing his eyes. "I got like two hours sleep."

"Why?" I ask.

"Well, do I have a story for you!" I'm intrigued, as Luke looks like he has been awake most of the night. "You know how the monks were in here praying?"

"Yeah."

"Well, when the last monk left the cave at about 10pm, he didn't turn the light off. It was keeping me awake and I was like, 'Oh man, I'm gonna have to get up!'"

So I eventually got out of the tent, waddled over and turned the light off. Then I took a few steps back and when I stepped back I trod barefoot into something sticky. I was like, '*What* is that?'" Luke is such a great story teller and already he has me drawn in.

"Then I looked down and I had absolutely no idea what it was. I couldn't figure it out! So I got down on my hands and knees to look at it closely. Looking at it with my torchlight I could see it was black and had small white dots in it. I still had no idea what I'd stepped in. I looked at the bottom of my foot and picked up a leaf from the floor to wipe it off but it was like tar. It was disgusting! It wouldn't come off and I'm thinking, 'What on *earth* is this?'"

So then as I'm down on my hands and knees looking at this goo I realise there is only one place it could have come from ..." I can see where this story is going and I giggle when I say, "Above?'"

" Yep. So I look up and the roof is *covered in bats*! I was fully shocked. I thought, 'Oh my goodness I've fully stepped in *bat poo*!' As soon as I realised I'd stepped in bat poo my mind started to race. I was like, 'Oh my gosh, bats have *rabies*. The poo probably has rabies in it. Oh my gosh, does my foot have a *cut*?!' I couldn't tell if my foot had a cut because this black *gooey* stuff was covering my foot, but I do have blisters and they are like open wounds. So, then I'm fully *freaking out* thinking I'm gonna get some sort of disease I don't even know about, from bats."

The picture Luke is creating is so real, so funny that tears are starting to roll down my cheeks.

Luke continues, "So then I had to come back to the tent and it was like I was in a Mario game jumping and avoiding obstacles, just to make sure I didn't step in any more of the bat poo splattered on the cave floor."

"How big was the patch you stepped in?" I ask.

"The spot I stepped in was the biggest by far. It was about the size of my palm. That's how much poo had been pooped in the same spot. Anyway, I got back to the tent and wanted to get the stuff off my foot first, but it was almost impossible. Using toilet paper, I had to scrape at it for five to ten minutes. I couldn't get it all off. To deal with the remainder

I put dirt on it so at least it wouldn't be sticky anymore. I got back into the tent and as I was lying there, I realised I could hear *noises*. It dawned on me that there were bats flying around inside the cave! And *you* were asleep while I lay beside you freaking out!"

I want to say sorry but I'm occupied with my laughter.

"I could hear the splat sounds of poo landing and realised that not only were bats pooing from the roof but they were *above* our tent as well! So we were suddenly in no man's land and a bomb of bat poo could land on our tent. So then I'm freaking out that one of the bats is going to poo on our tent. So I'm lying here freaking out and as I think about it more, I'm remembering that our tent doesn't have the *fly* on it. It's just the thin, net-like material of the tent."

We had thought we were genius when we decided to use the tent as a mosquito net. "The bat poo could goop straight through it. So I'm thinking poo is going to land on our faces, in our mouths, eyes! I even lay on my side but then I was worried poo would land in my ear! Meanwhile I keep hearing this dull thud of poo landing every couple of minutes. By now it was like 1am but I couldn't stop thinking about it all."

I kinda feel bad that I was asleep this whole time, but I'm enjoying the story too much.

"Then I realised that the bats were going to poo on our stuff that we had left outside the tent. My shoes were outside! So now, I was possibly gonna have poo in my shoe, or on my bag or whatever else we left out there. I think I finally got to sleep at about 3am. Then the monks woke me at 5am when they came back to the cave to pray."

I've pretty much been in stitches laughing the entire

time Luke has been telling me this story. The idea of his going through all this, while I lay peacefully beside him blissfully unaware, is too funny. I guess the marvel of sleeping in a cave is not as marvellous in reality. In reality, bats live in caves. I'm just glad it wasn't me who stepped in their poo.

We get out of the tent to check our stuff. I have to stifle my laughter as Luke discovers not only has bat poo landed on the tent but also on his bag and in his shoe. Seems my stuff is bat poo free! It's so funny watching Luke try to scrape this disgusting black poo off his shoe. I'm sure he will laugh about it in the future, but for now, I seem to be the only one laughing.

The monks have been up and about since 5am, but haven't yet gone on their alms collection. Luke goes for a toilet trip and comes back to tell me that the lumpy head monk has told him, through actions, that apparently the monks will go alms collecting, come back and eat, and then we can eat what is left over. The promise of a belly full of breakfast is too good to refuse. So, even though these monks don't depart the wat till 7am, we decide to wait around anyway. We don't expect to have to walk too far today so a late start shouldn't matter. We slowly pack our stuff while we wait for the monks to return. When they do return, they take a long time to eat. So much so that I worry that Luke misunderstood the monk and we are in fact waiting for nothing. Sitting out of sight seems the right thing to do as monks are not allowed to eat with others. I feel like I've been sitting here for an eternity. My stomach is grumbling and I can feel myself getting moody already. We haven't even started walking yet. Not a good sign. Finally the monks set up their leftover food for us. I'm so thankful. With the way my body is coping these days, I know that a full breakfast will start me off positively. I honestly don't know how the POWs marched on empty stomachs. Food is not only an energy giver but a morale lifter. My morale is definitely lifted by the rice, bamboo shoot, egg, pineapple and fish we feast on this morning.

Before we leave, the tubby monk takes a photo of us with his camera. We take one as well. It's a fantastic photo. Inside the cave the monk sits on a wooden bench while Luke and I sit on the blue tiled floor. In the background is the cave wall and Buddha statues. It doesn't give the real picture but it will be a reminder of the best temple we stayed at. We are sad to say goodbye. The monks form a farewell party to see us off. Lumpy head monk and tubby monk are amongst the group in their orange robes that wave to us as we walk down the highway. Big smiles and big hearts; I can tell they have loved having us at their temple. The heat out on the road is already intense. It's 9am which is much later than we like to start walking, but this wat has been fantastic and we had to make the most of it. I realise I never asked what the name of the wat was.

So I run back to ask, "Cheu ... wat?"

In unison they all reply, "Tâm Sukow!"

Of course, 'tâm'. I recall our friend Max the Monk from Wat Lum Sum – he taught me that Thai word for 'cave'. I wave goodbye to our monk friends again and run back to catch up with Luke.

19

Beauty

"Enjoy the little things,
for one day you may look back
and realise they were the big things."
Robert Brault

The end of this adventure is close. I can almost sense it. We aren't sure when we will reach Sangkhla Buri but know it will be in a day or two. It's incredible to think we have walked almost 300km so far.

I've witnessed a few disturbing sights this morning. Firstly, as I plodded along I noticed a man pull over on his motorbike on the other side of the road and get off. Walking up to a heap on the road, he picked up what was a dead dog. He then proceeded to tie that dead dog to the back of his motorbike with a two metre rope. Then, as if it was completely normal, he drove off dragging the dog along behind him.

Also, a road side food stall which we stopped at for a rest, had a pet monkey. There is something distressing about seeing a wide eyed, cowering primate chained up for the pleasure of humans. A monkey should be swinging through the trees, munching on fruit and doing monkey things. Thailand is infamous for its treatment of animals. Unfortunately, tourism encourages it. Walk down the main tourist street of Phuket, Koh Samui or Bangkok and you will find a local holding an iguana, monkey and worst of all, baby elephants.

Naive tourists get excited about the sight of an exotic animal and accept the snake around their neck or monkey in their arms for a 'once in a lifetime' photo. Unfortunately, they rarely take the time to consider what the life of this animal might be like. They don't appreciate what is happening. Most likely this animal they are holding has been drugged. This explains the calm nature and droopy eyes of the creature that, in reality, is often brutal and dangerous.

There is a local bar owner in Bangkok who is completely against the use of baby elephants as a source of tourism. I'm proud to know this man. Whenever he sees a terrified elephant being walked down the road, amongst the bright street lights, loud cars and masses of people, he holds up his hand made sign 'NO STREET ELEPHANTS!' Handing out pamphlets to nearby tourists, he is passionate about educating everyone as to why elephants should not be in the city. He discourages people from having their photos taken with the poor animals.

Even thinking back to Kanchanaburi, I remember seeing a chained up leopard for people to have their photos taken with. It is really upsetting. I wanted to let this particular poor little monkey go free, but I couldn't. Instead I had to hope that at least his owners treat him kindly.

∞ ∞

Walking past the 11km mark for the day, Luke and I realise we had expected the wat to be here, but there is no wat in sight. Worried we have missed it, we stop in a small village to ask about the local wat. Despite this village being *smack bang* on the highway, they are obviously very rural people. They cannot understand a word we are saying, even when we speak in Thai! Okay, so my Thai isn't great but the locals have been understanding us. These people have no idea what I'm saying. Maybe they are Burmese? Eventually they understand the word *wat* and point back the way we came. Confused, we turn back and spot a village 500m down the road at the bottom of a hill. There is a man standing on the highway waiting for a bus. We ask him where the wat is and he points at the village. Taking a closer look, we realise the large white un-wat looking building at the top of the village is actually a wat. A monk comes to the window and Luke and I sigh with relief. Calling to the monk who remains at the window, "Norn lup ... wat?", I'm surprised by his response. He isn't interested in us. I try again but he says something in Thai, points further down the village and walks away. Luke calls out again but it doesn't work. We have just been rejected for the first time by a wat. I can't believe it! What are we going to do? I don't want to walk any further as we know there are no more wats within walking distance today.

Luke and I walk into the village and stand on the dirt road. We stand there for a long time looking at each other, looking at the village, looking at the wat. I notice we are standing in front of quite a nice looking house. Completely made of wood, it looks elegant and welcoming. There is a map of the village on the verandah and I wonder to myself if this is the head man's house. Possibly that is what the monk had been saying to us. But once again, who really knows?

"Shall we give this house a go?" I ask Luke.

"It's our only option really," Luke replies.

Approaching the house, we can't see any sign of life. The house is on stilts and, not wanting to climb the stairs without permission, we stand on tip toes to try and see if anyone is inside. I notice that the television is on and there is, in fact, a person lying on the floor. "Sawadee ka!" I call out. The person looks up, quite obviously shocked to see two smelly *farang* standing outside her house. As she gets up to come outside, I realise she is a teenager.

A pretty, timid girl who has been quietly watching television has just had her world turned upside down. Her English, we find out, is extremely limited. It takes us about twenty minutes to explain to her what we are doing, why we are here and what we need. She is fascinated by the maps that we show her, though I'm not convinced she understands our story.

Eventually she confirms, "Norn lup?" pointing to her house.

In Thai, I say, "Koon oh-kay mai?" (Is that okay with you?)

She smiles shyly and nods. I ask her name and she replies, "Beauty."

It's so fitting. This girl *is* beautiful with long black, silky hair and delicate, smooth Thai features.

Climbing the stairs and taking a seat on the floor, Beauty brings us a fan and cold water.

"Kao?" Beauty asks. We had eaten lunch not long ago

and aren't very hungry, but we say 'yes' anyway. Beauty then says "ah-hahn?" No idea what it means, we just nod and smile. She looks at us curiously and wanders off leaving us to take in our surroundings. The room we sit in is bare; a television is the only thing in the room besides the token Buddhist shrine. The doors are wide open looking out onto the village life outside. It is an authentic, remote Thai village and I love it.

Beauty seems to be taking a while and we start to worry that we aren't being brought some fruit but an entire meal. We get the Thai phrase book and look up the word she said, *ah-hahn*, and find out it means 'meal'. I'm absolutely not hungry. When Beauty brings out a massive bowl of rice, a huge omelette and bamboo shoot curry I realise there is no way we are going to be able to finish it all. There is enough food here for a family. We don't finish it and feel really bad when Beauty comes to collect the dishes. To make matters worse she says, "ah-hahn glahng wun," pointing to the food we just ate. Followed by, "ah-hahn yen," which I have a horrible feeling means lunch and dinner, respectively. The Thai phrase book confirms this. Looks like we will be eating *another* meal in a few hours.

Beauty asks us to follow her. We are shown two bedrooms. One is for Luke and the other is for me. I realise that she is giving us *their* rooms. I'm really taken aback. We turned up on the doorstep of this girl's house and, without permission from her parents, we have been given food and a room to sleep in. When Beauty hands me a fresh bath towel I want to cry. I've been using a small travel towel, so holding a proper towel is just too overwhelming. I'm realising how much I take for granted at home. I have a wash and when I come back Luke is on the house phone. I hear him saying, "We are walking from Kanchanaburi to Sangkhla Buri. We were on the highway and we saw we were in a remote area. We thought we'd better find somewhere to sleep before it got dark, so we were wondering if we could stay here?"

When Luke gets off the phone he says, "Beauty obviously hadn't fully understood us. The man on the phone said, 'Hello, apparently you are having some communication problems?' I explained our story to him. He told Beauty. They are fine with us staying, so that's good news."

Without warning the skies open and torrential rain consumes the village. Two boys come running into the house accompanied by a young guy. Drenched to the bone and covering their school bags in plastic, they look at us curiously. The anticipation of playing in the rain supersedes any wonder they had about the *farang*. In minutes, the two boys are in their undies frolicking in the downpour along with Beauty and Non, who is their older brother. I'm mildly jealous of how much fun they are having. As I watch them laugh and splash in the puddles, I contemplate how different our lives are from these simple village folk. City life takes the child out of you, forcing you to think and behave accordingly. Meanwhile, I can't remember the last time I deliberately went out in the rain simply to play in it.

Beauty and Non's parents arrive home and their father is very surprised to find *farang* in his house. He doesn't speak a word of English but shakes our hands, smiles brightly and speaks rapidly to us in Thai. The introduction has left me feeling welcomed and the father bounds off to do his fatherly duties. It feels like we only just ate lunch but before we know it, dinner is ready. We eat with the children while the adults eat separately. I feel a part of this family immediately. The two boys are being cheeky; Beauty is pulling them into line, and Non is chatting to us with his limited English. The father comes over to give us a plate of meat. He is very enthusiastic and urges us to try it. Taking a piece, I find the meat to be chewy, unlike anything I've eaten before. Since Non speaks a bit of English, we try to find out from him what we are eating.

"It like a snake," Non says.

"It's like a snake?" Trying to think what might be like a snake I ask, "Is it on the ground or in trees?"

"Yes."

"Okay ..."

"It eat ant!" Non exclaims.

"Okay ... is it a frog?" I'm stumped, what have we just eaten?

"No," Non replies, trying desperately to remember the word for the creature in English.

"Snake?" Luke trys.

"No."

"Is it a lizard?" I say. Non looks at me confused. It seems he doesn't know the word *lizard*. The Thai phrase book, as usual, is failing us at a time we when need it. The word lizard is not in there, but after asking the same questions a number of times, Luke and I both decide it has to be lizard we have just eaten.

Using the Thai phrase book, we try and have some conversations with them. Beauty and Non are extremely patient as we literally look up each individual word to try and construct sentences. We laugh and joke all night. It's so great to be amongst a family again. Getting all our maps out, we show the family the route we have walked. They are in awe – and so am I. Tomorrow is our last big day of walking. As I look at the maps with brown edges stained from my sweaty hands, ripped and worn, I think back to when we purchased them in Bangkok. Crisp new paper maps that we had to fold ourselves; promised adventure and new experiences. That is exactly what we have had. This trip began as a walk in honour of the POWs of WWII but it became so much more than that. This expedition became about the people we met along the way.

Luke and I decide to go to bed. We are tired and want to get walking early tomorrow. The family understands and as they set up their mattresses in the TV room, I stand and watch this rural family that opened up their lives to us today. Beauty gives me a set of pyjamas to wear to bed. I retire to what is her room, change into her clothes and slip into her bed. These small acts of kindness overwhelm me and I burst into tears. Sitting beneath a mosquito net in the depth of rural Thailand, I allow all the emotion that I've held within to pour out of me. The people of Thailand have impacted me in a huge way. They have taught me about generosity, trust, humanity, kindness and opening yourself to others. By Luke and I allowing ourselves to meet people along the way, we have found our lives enriched by their hospitality. It has caused me to look within myself and aim to become a better person. I cry myself to sleep as I bask in the awesomeness of this expedition and the sadness of its almost being over.

∞ ∞

I am standing by the river. The Warrior of Light is with me.

I can see the people standing on the riverbank opposite. The Warrior of Light takes my hand and says, "It is time." We cross the river and suddenly I can see all their faces.

They are all here: Mai, Patrick, Max the Monk, Wireke, Surathin, Beauty and Non. Some of their names I don't know, but I know their faces: the monk from Ban Kao, the locals who fed us at Wat Phu Toei Samakkahi Tharp near Hell Fire Pass, the family we stayed with by the dam, the monks at Tâm Sukow. Every person we have stayed with, who has fed us and who we met along the walk, is here.

They are all standing side by side along the river. As I walk past them, I give each person a hug and tell them, "Thank you," again. At the end stands Luke and he is pointing to a person in the distance. Though his face is blurred, I know exactly who it is — Tom. He is sitting outside a beautiful old church up on a hill. I recognise it because I've been there before. This time he isn't holding an engagement ring. He is holding my heart.

I try to run but something is holding me back. I turn to look at The Warrior of Light. "My child, you are almost there. But you are not quite ready yet."

"What must I do?"

"You must finish the race before you. Take yesterday's pain and turn it into today's strength."

I look back at the faces of my new found friends. Their lessons of life have changed me more than they will ever realise. I look back at Tom and whisper, "I'm coming soon."

20

The End of the Road

"When you think about it,
probably some of the best things
that ever happened to you in life,
happened because you said Yes to something.
Otherwise, things just sort of stay the same."
Danny Wallace

Beauty's mother pulls some flowers off a tree, hands them to me and says, "Dom." The sweet fragrance fills my nostrils as I bury my nose in them.

"Chock dee," she says.

I look at Non, "Chock dee?"

"Good luck!" he translates.

I smile at the sweet gesture of this wonderful woman. I don't want to leave. I'm really sad to be saying goodbye. Of all the people we have said goodbye to, Beauty and her family are the hardest to depart from. The entire family stands on their verandah to wave us goodbye. I choke back my tears as we walk up the village road and back to the highway.

Luke and I walk in silence. Today is a big day. Today is the end. When we arrive at the bridge that marks our approach to Sangkhla Buri, we find it manned by uniformed guards. They are stopping every car that is coming from the north. Nervously we approach them but there is no need to fear. They cheerfully call out, "Sawadee kup!" as we walk by.

After the bridge we discover that we have some massive mountains to tackle. Thankfully, by an act of God, the sun is not out today. The weather is actually overcast and drizzling. I'm thankful, as I'm not sure I could have done this in the normal conditions where the humid air prevents our sweat from evaporating. The mountains are monstrous. The highway is going directly up one side of a mountain in one steep ascent and then down the other side in one direct steep descent. My knees are killing me. To make it to the top, I have to look down and focus each thought, breath and burst of energy on moving forward up the hill. It's absolute torture.

Luke is ahead of me all day and stops to wait every half hour or so. I'm thankful for the time alone. I need the space to think, reminisce and pray. I think back to those days on Skype when we couldn't even come up with an idea. Here we are approaching the end of an expedition that we created, planned and executed ourselves. This is what adventure is about; two people exploring, persevering and accomplishing their dream.

It's been an incredible few weeks and when I reach the top of one of the many mountains I've climbed today, I can see Sangkhla Buri for the first time. It's a humbling moment as this is the sight I've been waiting for.

"That's it, Rachel. Sangkhla Buri ..." Luke says to me when I reach him.

"We walked all the way here, it's crazy," I say as we stand and take in the view of Sangkhla Buri and all it means for us.

Sangkhla Buri is the end of the road for us. It was also the end of the road for our friend Stan. He was forced to walk 300km from Ban Pong to Sangkhla Buri. We have done this for him and every other POW. I can see the pagoda of Wat Wang Wiwekaram far in the distance. The gold paint stands out against the green backdrop of the jungle canopy. It is on the far side of town and, for me, it symbolises the end of our journey.

"Ready to keep going?" Luke asks me.

"Sure am." Now that I've seen the end, I've found a new energy on the road. The strong sense of accomplishment and pride that I'm feeling is overpowering. I honestly can't believe we have walked all the way here.

As we make the final descent into town, the rain arrives. For the last time, I put on my rain poncho and allow the drops of water to career down my forehead and into my eyes. It's hiding the tears. I take note of every single thing we are walking past. I love walking. The slowness of it allows you to truly take in the world around you; the toughness of it makes you realise just how much you can endure; the openness of it gives you opportunity to experience the world and its people; the rawness of it ensures you meet the elements head on. I wouldn't have done this journey any other way. Walking allowed us to see Thailand in all its authenticity; I have fallen in love with tapioca fields, rubber sheets hanging out to dry and toothless smiles that offer us a lift. I'm going to miss getting up each day, and walking.

We pass by a wat right on the outskirts of Sangkhla

Buri. A big reclining Buddha paints an impressive picture. His expression conveys infinite love and wisdom. These have become such familiar sights but still fascinate me. I feel the Buddha's eyes burning into me as though my arrival has been anticipated. We are tempted to go inside the temple, ask one last time, 'Norn lup?' but we don't. We have made it to Sangkhla Buri. There are two kilometres left and we are going to walk those today.

We are exhausted. Our bodies are tired, blistered feet, throbbing shoulders and aching hips. We are fatigued not having had a proper sleep in weeks. Our sunburn has turned to a heavy tan – only our clothing has protected us and we could win a competition for the worst t-shirt tan in history. Despite these things, our bodies have carried us across the finish line. I'm impressed with the human body. It can endure a lot, but I'm aware that my body is in desperate need of rest. As we drag our feet into the town of Sangkhla Buri with our heads held high, I look around. No-one is here to meet us. No-one knows what we have just completed. No-one knows the significance of this day, except each other, but then I hear a familiar voice, "Hello!"

I turn to find Non standing outside a mechanics smiling at us. "Non!" Luke and I yell in unison. It's fantastic to see a familiar face. It turns out Non works in Sangkhla Buri. We had no idea. With Non's assistance we find a place to stay, P Guesthouse, which will be our home for the next few days as we recover. I walk into our twin room and flop onto the bed. I fall asleep immediately.

∞ ∞

I don't know how long I've been here. All I know is that I feel like death. I can hear myself groaning but I can't help it. I'm in pain. *I open my eyes and find that my room is filled with men. I can see their ribs poking through their thin, pasty skin. Their eyes have sunk into their face so much that they look like skeletons. Living skeletons. I realise it is the POWs. They don't say anything, they simply stand and watch me.* Suddenly the door swings open and Luke comes rushing in. I jump up and realise I'm covered in sweat. The POWs disappear and I register that I'm alone in the room.

"Are you okay?" Luke asks, his face filled with concern. "You've been moaning really loudly for ages." I groan as my stomach churns and then tightens. I think I might throw up.

"I'm not feeling well ..." I moan, lying back down on the bed.

"Can I get you anything?"

"Water, I just want water."

My body is falling apart bit by bit. I'm running a fever, my stomach is cramping and I'm so, so thirsty. I can't move. I can't eat. All I can do is lie here, and moan.

∞ ∞

"How long have I been asleep?" I ask Luke as I join him on our dainty cabin verandah.

"About a day I guess."

"I remember your coming in and asking if I wanted to go and have dinner. There was no way I was gonna eat last night though."

"Yeah, you didn't seem very well."

"I think my body must have just, fallen apart. It kept going for as long as it needed to but when it was allowed to stop for good, it knew it. I'm feeling pretty weak." I put my face in my hands and take some deep breaths.

"I'm hungry now though. Want to come with me to get something to eat?" I ask Luke.

"Yep."

Sangkhla Buri, I discover, is a small Thai town surrounded by beautiful jungle. It is way off the tourist trail which means that it's a great place for us to debrief and re-adjust to *normal* life again. There are a few westerners about but most of them are volunteers at the Baan Unrak Children's Village which supports disadvantaged women and children. Generally the town is pretty quiet and I enjoy walking down our little street. Already it feels like home.

Our guesthouse sits on the shore of the dam and we can see Wat Wang Wiwekaram on the opposite bank and Saphan Mon Bridge to our right. A spectacular sight, the bridge is 400m long and is the longest hand-constructed bridge in Thailand. The view from our verandah is incredibly romantic and it makes me miss Tom. I was unable to call him in the last few days of the walk due to there being no reception. Therefore, he was very surprised when I rang him to say we had finished the walk. He hadn't seen that coming.

The routine of sleeping in, journalling and reading in the morning, walking to the market for lunch and relaxing for the rest of the day, is just what I need. So much has happened over the past few weeks, I need the time and space to cogitate.

Sitting on our verandah is a great place for reflection and I'm spending a lot of time here journalling and looking back over this experience. I gain a lot from nature, and the panoramic view I have of the wat, bridge and dam is the inspiration I need. The walk took us twenty one days; seventeen days of walking and four rest days. I flick through my journal and skim my notes. I read something I wrote down so long ago I had forgotten it.

I turn to Luke who is sitting next to me, "Hey, we did this walk in the same amount of time as the POWs, minus our rest days."

"That's awesome!" Luke replies.

"Also, they did their forced march in April/May just like we did. I don't remember knowing that."

"Me either! Pretty awesome though," Luke says.

Despite having now walked the distance, I still have no idea how the POWs survived their march. The conditions they walked in were atrocious: starvation, beatings, sleep deprivation, infection. Their hell supersedes ours by a hundredfold. I could have left it all behind at any time to return to three full meals a day, air conditioning, cleanliness, safety, sanity. The POWs couldn't. Having now experienced the terrain and the elements, I cannot believe anyone survived the 300km and arrived into Sangkhla Buri alive. Luke and I were not trying to recreate the POWs experience. We wanted to understand, even if just a little, what they went through.

This expedition was in memory of the F Force soldiers: Stan's working party who walked the 300km from Ban Pong to Sangkhla Buri, in Thailand. There is no doubt that the F Force were the worst hit of all the groups that worked on the railway. They had the worst accommodation, living in the mud and never ending rain of the wet season. They were the furthest in distance from the base camp, which meant getting food supplies to them was difficult. They suffered malaria, dysentery and cholera which resulted in their having the highest death toll for a force on the railway. Those who did survive continued to suffer, as the traumatic experiences they had whilst being POWs on the infamous Thai-Burma railway haunted them for the rest of their lives. Every step I have taken has been for them.

I giggle when I read in my journal the phrase, 'Where you going?' We were asked that question thousands of times. Sometimes it was just an inquisitive local but other times it was someone offering us a lift. We were offered fifty one lifts in seventeen days. When you think about it, that is pretty incredible. The generosity of the locals has astounded me. More than willing to help out a stranger, the Thai people have gone above and beyond what I ever would have expected. People sought us out to offer us lifts, food and directions. Others have found us on their doorsteps and welcomed in strangers with odd requests. All of them have opened up their lives to us.

We stayed in eight temples; some fed us, some socialised with us and all put a roof over our heads. I have a new found respect for Buddhism. Every time I see a monk, I will be reminded of all the friends I have in temples scattered over Thailand. It's been fascinating to spend time with these monks and gain an understanding of what their life entails.

Their devotion and discipline is something to be admired. I hope that when people witness me and my faith, I will display such qualities as well.

The reality of travelling to a foreign land is that we can't observe another culture without finding a mirror reflecting back on oneself. I've learnt more about myself on this trip than I wanted to. Being forced to look deep within oneself is uncomfortable. I wasn't entirely proud of what I found. I discovered things about myself that I don't like; I'm selfish, controlling and demanding. These are things I want to, and can, change about myself. During the walk I didn't feel ready to delve into that scary reality. It was too much, but now that I'm on the other side of this adventure and preparing to go home – I'm ready.

I couldn't have predicted that my life would change so drastically on this trip. I came to Thailand believing I would learn about the POWs, the Death Railway and about whether I was strong enough to do a 300km walk. However, as much as I observed the locals, I equally observed myself. I found that I was forced to have confidence in myself when I felt I had none. I had to trust in my capabilities though I had no proof I was able. I've learnt that the human spirit is tough. It is like rubber; it expands when put through extreme conditions but can return to its original form in no time. I guess this is one reason the POWs did survive – the strength of the human spirit.

We rocked up on the doorsteps of three houses during the walk and imposed ourselves on the people living there. We were never turned away. We were always offered beds, food and friendship. I can't say I would do the same if someone turned up on my doorstep. So often we are taught in the west to be afraid. Don't trust the world or the people in it. Question everything and everyone.

Luke and I threw ourselves out into this big, bad world and hoped for the best. I remember how terrified I was in Bangkok. Were we doing the right thing? Would we be okay? Where would we sleep? What would we do if something went wrong? Turns out, we were more than okay. Turns out, when you open yourself up to the world, it gives you so much more in return. It gave me an exceeding amount of joy, an abundance of hope and a new found faith in humanity. Yes, there are bad people out there and you do have to be aware, but the majority of the world is kind and friendly. The majority of the world wants to be your friend.

Just like the people we have met along this journey, I want to be kind to strangers; I want to seek out ways to help another human being. In the Bible there is a well known parable of 'The Good Samaritan'. Jesus tells the story of a traveller who was beaten, robbed and left for dead. A priest and Levite both pass this man and ignore him. It is not until a Samaritan, who is technically the traveller's enemy, passes by that the man gets assistance. The world wants me to see every one as my enemy until proven otherwise, but I will no longer look at the world with the same eyes. I have experienced the goodness of people.

The Thai's are incredibly generous. They assisted the POWs during the war and many of them died doing so. They are a people that will go above and beyond, no matter what. I'm sad to have witnessed what tourism has done to the cities and tourist hot-spots of Thailand. These areas are losing the spark that the real Thailand exhibits. The Thai people I have met are happy and content. They live simple lives in the countryside and that is enough for them. It is easy to see why they are happy with what they have. For it seems what they have at any given moment is enough.

I'm reminded again of another scripture from the Bible. Paul writes,

> 'I've learned by now to be quite content whatever my circumstances. I'm just as happy with little as with much, with much as with little. I've found the recipe for being happy whether full or hungry, hands full or hands empty. Whatever I have, wherever I am, I can make it through anything in the One who makes me who I am."

(Philippians 4: 12-13, The Message)

There is something to be said for people who have learned the promise of a content life. One thing is for sure, material goods do not bring happiness. What does bring happiness is family, friends and love. These have been tested for me during this journey and I believe I'm coming out as a stronger person who values these three things more than ever. I have spent the last month living my dream, but so often I found that even though I was exactly where I wanted to be and doing exactly what I wanted to be doing, I missed Tom more than ever, and simply couldn't wait to get home.

∞ ∞

It's midday. Luke and I are walking to the local market for lunch. A car pulls over and inside is a British couple. They ask us if we would like to come to Three Pagoda Pass with them. I look at Luke, "I'd love to visit it seeing as we are so close! We could have lunch there?" Next thing we are on our way to the border of Thailand and Burma. The chance meeting turns out to be a much needed encouragement. Tom and Lynda are retired and have moved to Thailand because their sons live out here. One of their sons runs an NGO in Sangkhla Buri for Burmese children who live across the border in Thailand but have no access to Thai benefits.

"We are just heading to the markets to buy some furniture. There is really great, cheap wooden products sold at this border. What brings you to Thailand?" says Lynda.

We tell this couple all about our journey; what, why, how. It's almost like a debrief session. The opportunity to talk to someone, besides each other, about this incredible experience is just what we need. Tom and Lynda are intrigued and ask us many questions. It's fantastic.

The famous three pagodas are much smaller than I expected. White in colour with gold and red ribbon draped around them, they sit in the middle of a roundabout. Considering how highly they are regarded, they seem small in significance. At the border crossing where people are going into Burma, soldiers armed with rifles watch on as Tom and Lynda leave us to explore. They will pick us up again in one hour. Luke and I meander through the markets which are situated along the Thai/Burma border, looking at all the souvenirs for sale.

In amongst the stalls, we find a bronze plaque that commemorates the thousands of Australian prisoners who died during the construction of the Thai-Burma railway. It is a reminder that though our journey may be over, for the POWs, it wasn't over by any means. The plaque also marks the site of where this section of the railway originally stood. Now all that stands are these market stalls and a view into neighbouring Burma.

In between two of the market stalls, I notice a simple gate. As I study it closer, I realise on the other side of this gate is Burma. Border security isn't as strict as it claims to be at the crossing we had just passed a mere three hundred metres up the road. Entering Burma *could* be as simple as opening a gate that sits for all to see at the market. All it would need is for someone to take the risk, open it and walk through.

Epilogue

"The traveller sees what he wants to see.
The tourist sees what he has come to see."
G.K.Chesterton

Squeezing into our seats on an overfilled minivan, I contemplate the fact that a walk that took us twenty one days is now going to be an effortless six hour drive. The road coming out of Sangkhla Buri is incredibly windy and I am nauseous from the erratic driving. In a vehicle it is so much more obvious just how dangerous these roads are. I can't quite believe we walked them. Even more so, I can't believe we survived.

When we reach the bridge that takes us out of Sangkhla Buri, the uniformed guards check everyone's passport. It's only now that Luke and I realise that they are checking for illegal Burmese. It was only a few days ago that these guards greeted us cheerfully as we walked by.

About half of the route from Sangkhla Buri to Bangkok is the road we walked on. It is a strange feeling to be seeing it all again from the window of a speeding vehicle. I remember every corner, every road side stall, every town. It all contains memories. In a vehicle, the scenery flashes by before you have a chance to appreciate it. What I'd give to be walking these roads again.

∞ ∞

It's time to say goodbye. After five weeks together Luke is about to fly back to Sydney while I'm going home to London later this evening. It hasn't been easy living so closely together. We have fought and struggled with each other's differences, but ultimately we have tested our relationship and survived. That is what matters.

Bangkok seems empty without Luke. I wander the streets feeling out of place. Stall owners hassle me to buy their mass produced bogus t-shirts and jewellery. I see a poor innocent tourist being swindled into a 10B tuk-tuk ride. Little does he know he is about to be driven around jewellery shops and tailors as the driver tries to earn his commission. I miss being out on the road. All of our new found friends are on my mind. They were never out to trick me. Here in Bangkok I'm already questioning everyone that approaches me. Everyone speaks English – it's just not the same.

I still love Bangkok though; cheap mango shakes, curries and nutella pancakes. These stalls are my favourite and I make the most of all of them before I head to the airport for my flight home.

∞ ∞

I can see him. Though his face is so familiar, I feel like

I'm seeing him for the first time. He smiles; that big, wide smile I love so much. I run towards him through the crowds of people waiting for loved ones, drop my bag and jump into a big, much needed hug.

We start to walk away, hand in hand, and I can't help but stare. I take in all his features; his big brown eyes, huge smile, overgrown hair and mis-matched clothes.

"You look so ... different," I say.

"So do you! Weird hey ..." Tom replies.

I feel like I'm on a first date, nervous, shy and excited. The simple act of holding his hand is making my heart flutter.

Then Tom reaches into his pocket and pulls out a kinder egg.

∞ ∞

I have realised my dream and for a brief time have been privileged to live the life I've always wanted to live – the life of an adventurer. I have followed in the footsteps of those gone before me despite what it promised; hardship, pain and risk. I accepted these consequences of my choice to walk, in return for the promise of the unknown. I walked day in and day out in memory of those who did not have the choice. I walked for them. I persevered because they persevered. I come to the end of this journey knowing that I have stood beside my brother, a sister with faults. I have been a million miles away from my husband, a wife with crazy dreams who asked a lot from him. Now I return with a new knowledge of myself – as a sister, wife and friend.

Acknowledgements

I had a dream to complete an expedition and to write a book. I have succeeded in doing both! The achievement of these two aspirations of mine has not been completed alone.

Thank you to Stan. Your war experiences were horrific. Your life was a testament to forgiveness and hope. We walked for you. I wrote this book because of you.

Thank you to my parents who read, re-read and edited this book. Without them I'm afraid it wouldn't have been a book worth reading.

Thank you to Jon Maxwell who designed the fantastic cover of this book.

Thank you to Tom. Two months after our wedding I embarked on an expedition that kept us apart for five weeks. Thanks for being supportive of my dreams and ambitions.

Thank you to Luke for joining me on this expedition. It was a true adventure. We wanted to do an expedition that would push us beyond our limits. It did that and more. We were tested, but we made it.

Most importantly I have to thank and acknowledge my brother Rohan. I have two brothers, Luke and Rohan. The three of us grew up in an era when playing outside was the norm. Our childhood was filled with adventure. As we got older we still craved this adventurous lifestyle. We would dream and scheme about doing an expedition together. But lack of communication and openness between us all meant Rohan was not included in our discussion about this particular trip. Therefore he didn't join us. For this, I am so sorry.

Completing this expedition taught me that the most important thing in life is people and relationships. In fact, all that truly matters in life is the people you have around you. Completing an expedition is incredible, life changing and eye opening. But if I had the choice between expeditions or family … I would choose family.

I will live with the regret of not including Rohan on this journey with us. It's no consolation, but this book is dedicated to Rohan.

My hope is that by reading this book all will be encouraged and inspired by the fact that anyone can go on an adventure. The essential part is that you lock in a start date. The only thing stopping you, is yourself.

Life is an adventure.
Rachel Beswetherick

Bibliography

Daws, Gavin, *Prisoners of the Japanese*. Great Britain: Simon & Schuster UK, 1994

Lomax, Eric, *The Railway Man*. New York: W. W. Norton, 1995

Braddon, Russell, *The Naked Island*. London: Pan Books Ltd, 1955

McCormack, Gavan & Nelson, Hank, *The Burma Thailand Railway*. Thailand, Silkworm Books, 1993

Lexus & Rough Guides, *The Rough Guide Phrasebook: Thai*. UK: Rough Guides, 2006

The Thai Burma Railway Centre in Kanchanaburi was also a great source of information.

For more information about the expedition

Visit the expedition website @
www.deathrailwaywalk.com

Visit Rachel's website @
www.intrepid-girl.com

4206220R00143

Printed in Great Britain
by Amazon.co.uk, Ltd.,
Marston Gate.